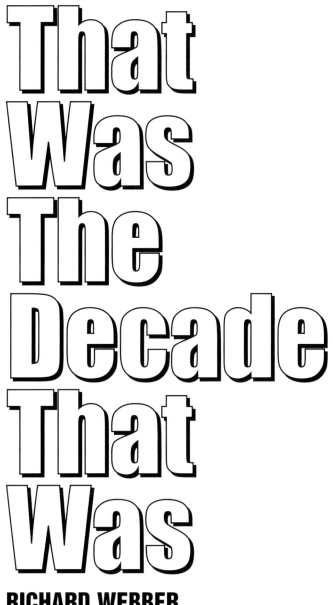

That Was The Decade That Was

RICHARD WEBBER

 MICHAEL O'MARA BOOKS LIMITED

First published in Great Britain in 2006 by
Michael O'Mara Books Limited
9 Lion Yard
Tremadoc Road
London SW4 7NQ

A CIP catalogue record for this book is available from the British Library

ISBN 1-84317-124-4

www.mombooks.com

Designed and typeset by Design 23

Printed and bound in Singapore by Tien Wah Press

CONTENTS

INTRODUCTION

The era of the swinging sixties was a liberating period in more ways than one. Leaving behind the shackles associated with post-war Britain, it was a time of freedom, adventure, hope, growing prosperity and increasing technological ingenuity. It was good riddance to the era of rations and rebuilding following the Second World War, and a warm welcome to an air of sunny optimism and expectation – and what a decade it became. There was a deluge of major achievements, from the introduction of the contraceptive pill to the increasing prosperity of the British public and, arguably, the decade's single greatest feat: the Moon landing in 1969.

In the world of television, it was an experimental, exciting time, not least because these were the years in which colour TV really took off and a new station, BBC2, was launched. When it came to commissioning new programmes, TV bosses were prepared to go with their hunches, allowing producers the chance to try out new shows without having to endure a series of cumbersome committees. Instead, a project could be green-lighted over a cup of coffee.

Some people criticize the quality of bygone television, disputing the claims that a 'golden era' ever existed. But let's face it, anything would be golden compared to the trash largely dished up today. Of course, if you sift carefully through today's TV schedules, you'll find some high-quality programmes: documentaries, news coverage, sporting events and period dramas frequently display superb broadcasting standards, and technical wizardry means we're seeing high-quality visual effects like never before. But, sadly, we're having to endure the age of depressing reality shows, banal makeover programmes and endless stories of people seeking better lives abroad – probably to escape such depressing TV. Surely it's nonsensical for broadcasters to believe that all that viewers want is more of the same? To top it all, television executives have the temerity to fill up other slots in the schedules with repeats of these cheaply produced shows and, ultimately, to revisit some of the gormless souls featured in the previous series. It's endless.

Compared to what we are offered now, the imagination and quality of sixties' television appears even more astonishing. Some people would still argue that television in the sixties was uneventful and rudimentary, especially in the genre of children's television, where the wires controlling puppet characters glistened in the studio lighting like beacons. But such claims are simply not true. Yes, technology inevitably imposed limitations, whereas today the box of tricks at the production team's fingertips is mind-boggling. But there is more to television than special effects and the sixties were halcyon days.

OPPOSITE: Pay TV 1960s-style involved a slot meter attached to the set, into which this little boy (watching *Andy Pandy*) had to drop a sixpence every hour.

If the fifties were the pioneering years, during which people began to come to terms with this relatively new medium as a vehicle for entertaining the masses, then television came of age during the sixties. The decade offered a freshness and buoyancy that bred a culture of experimentation and innovation. Many programmes were vibrant, adventurous and energetic. Of course, the quicksands of television are notoriously tricky to navigate, with many programmes gobbled up and thus lost without trace. Just like any period in the medium's history, the sixties also experienced its fair share of failures but, significantly, many programmes enjoyed a longevity that has led to them now being regarded as classics of their genre. Just think of all the shows originating during this era that are still showing today: *Coronation Street*, *Songs of Praise*, *Match of the Day*, *Top of the Pops*, *Gardeners' World* and *Holiday,* amongst others. Then there are those which are still repeated, including *Dad's Army* and *Steptoe and Son*; how many of today's programmes will still be transmitted in forty years' time?

The vaults of television stations are full of dust-covered film canisters containing milestones in the evolution of television entertainment dating back to this period. Take children's TV as an example: compared with today's fast-paced, action-packed programmes, the likes of *Trumpton* and *Tales of the Riverbank* may seem pedestrian and basic, but they'll always retain a gentle charm that is missing from much of today's programming. And it's not just children's television – the same applies to television shows across all genres. The sixties offered a treasure trove of goodies, from which some landmark productions emerged.

So, it's been a pleasure stepping back in time to review the medium from 1960 to 1969, revisiting some old favourites, unearthing more obscure programmes, interviewing many of the people behind the success of the shows and generally wallowing in nostalgia. This book isn't intended to be a comprehensive study of sixties TV. It's more an entertaining tour through some of the hits and the misses of the decade, a memory-provoking trip through a special period of British television, during which I've focused primarily on homegrown shows instead of the spate of imports, largely from the States, which began impacting on our screens.

Selecting which programmes to feature and which to leave out has been a difficult choice. To qualify for inclusion, the show had to have started in the sixties, although there are occasional exceptions. For example, in talking about the launch of ITV's *Magpie* I had to discuss its BBC rival, *Blue Peter*, even though *Blue Peter* started in the late fifties. But as a general rule, before considering a programme for the book, it had to have made its screen debut between 1960 and 1969. Obviously I haven't been able to include every show that emerged from this period, so some

people may be disappointed to find one or two of their own personal favourites missing. I hope, however, that those I have chosen to include will bring lots of happy memories rushing back. It's been a pleasant journey for me; I hope it is for you, too. Happy reading!

RICHARD WEBBER
MINEHEAD, SOMERSET – MAY 2005

CHILDREN'S TELEVISION

At times, we're probably all guilty of looking back on the children's television we grew up with through rose-tinted specs, but for many people, myself included, the sixties was *the* golden era. It is true that some of today's infants, seemingly computer-literate before they're out of nappies, are unlikely to be mesmerized by puppets made from ping-pong balls and foam, but if there has ever been a halcyon period in children's television, it must surely be the sixties, a rich and fruitful decade in which many of the programmes now regarded as classics were born.

OPPOSITE: Florence and Dougal first rode *The Magic Roundabout* in Britain in 1965.

BELOW: *Blue Peter* presenters Christopher Trace and Valerie Singleton with *Blue Peter* dog, Honey, in 1965.

By the dawn of the sixties, *Muffin the Mule* was heading out to grass while *The Woodentops* had sold their farm, retired to a bungalow on the south coast and were living the life of Riley on repeat fees that would line their pockets for years to come. Even *The Flowerpot Men*, those indefatigable twins who conversed in their indecipherable 'flobadob' language, had abandoned Weed and headed for pastures new, leaving behind a televisual legacy, like many of their contemporaries from the fifties, that would continue to entertain kids for decades.

This was, of course, an era when puppets were apparently proud to display a profusion of wires and strings sprouting from every extremity. Production standards were occasionally crude and, like any period in television's history, there was some early dross dished out in the form of entertainment. But so many offerings have retained their charm even today.

The pioneer responsible for several jewels from the period, most notably *Camberwick Green* (initially called *Candlewick Green* until a typing mistake in the BBC contract altered its name for ever), was Gordon Murray, who also gave us *Trumpton* and the lesser-known *Chigley*. Many people remember the little ditty, 'Pugh, Pugh, Barney McGrew, Cuthbert, Dibble

BELOW: Windy Miller and Mickey Murphy look on as Doctor Mopp is stopped by PC McGarry while driving through *Camberwick Green*.

and Grubb', and know they're the names of the intrepid fire crew, commanded by Captain Flack, who were always ready to respond to emergencies around the streets of *Trumpton*. Mind you, this was before emergency-service response times were as closely monitored as they are today, which is just as well, because the fire engine was agonizingly slow, and the most daunting incident the team encountered was rescuing a moggy from a tree. God knows how they would have coped if the biscuit factory at nearby *Chigley* was ablaze.

Gordon Murray's little worlds were idyllic: citizens lived in harmony and crime was non-existent. The cluster of puppets were perfect role models of politeness, typifying the society their creator once knew; Murray was also using the programmes as a way to encourage children to be kind and considerate to others. The words 'vandalism', 'mugging' and 'robbery' weren't even in the Trumptonshire dictionary. Murray, now in his eighties, recalls: 'Many years ago I saw a charming Czech puppet film set in a village, and thought what a splendid idea it would be to base a programme in a typical English village where only minor incidents occur.' In *Camberwick Green*, *Trumpton* and *Chigley* there was never a crisis, and citizens were amicable and co-operative. 'That is what I wanted children to be.' The feeling of serenity was palpable in Murray's productions, so much so that in *Trumpton* a dearth of fires meant the elderly fire-engine driver appeared to drive with his eyes shut. In the original promotional material, tucked away in the BBC archives, we learn that there hasn't been a serious fire in *Trumpton* for some thirty years, which is just as well because the stop-frame method of animation meant it was impossible to film smoke or flames, hence the reason the firemen earned their wages performing such perilous tasks as recovering hats and cats from trees.

Camberwick Green was first transmitted in 1966. Although only thirteen episodes were made (each taking a fortnight to create on a shoestring budget), it was repeated weekly throughout the year until, in 1967, it was joined in the schedules by *Trumpton*. This was set in a market town, yet *Trumpton* could hardly be described as 'bustling', its traffic-free roads leaving absolutely no need for any kind of congestion charge! Life in *Trumpton* centred on a square dominated by the town clock. When, in 1969, the opportunity arose for a third series, *Chigley*, a village just two miles from *Camberwick Green* and three from *Trumpton*, was born, knitting everything together neatly in the county of Trumptonshire. In all, thirty-nine oft-repeated episodes were made.

> 'Many years ago I saw a charming Czech puppet film set in a village, and thought what a splendid idea it would be to base a programme in a typical English village where only minor incidents occur.'

WHO'S WHO IN TRUMPTONSHIRE

Comprising of the villages of *Camberwick Green* and *Chigley*, both just a few miles from the sleepy town of *Trumpton*, the county of Trumptonshire was a rural idyll. But can you recall the names of the characters who walked the lanes of Trumptonshire?

CAMBERWICK GREEN RESIDENTS

Each episode of *Camberwick Green* began with the little verse, 'Here is a box, a musical box, wound up and ready to play. But this box can hide a secret inside. Can you guess what is in it today?' Then out would pop the character we'd shadow for that day – and there were many to choose from:

Mickey Murphy, the baker, and his children, Paddy and Mary
Windy Miller, who lived at Colley's Mill
Farmer Bell
PC McGarry
Captain Snort, Sergeant Major Grout and the soldiers at Pippin Fort
Mr Carraway, the fishmonger
Mrs Honeyman, the local rumourmonger
Peter Hazell, the postman
Mrs Dingle, the postmistress, and her puppy, Packet
Mr Crockett, who owned the garage
Doctor Mopp
Thomas Tripp, the milkman
Roger Varley, the chimney sweep
Mr Dagenham, the car salesman (appeared in only one episode)

CHIGLEY RESIDENTS

Over at *Chigley*, adventures normally took place at either Treddles Wharf, Winkstead Hall, the biscuit factory or Chigley Pottery.

Lord Belborough and his trusty old butler, Brackett
Mr Bilton, the gardener at Winkstead Hall
Mr Cresswell, manager at the biscuit factory
Mr Fletcher, biscuit-factory loading supervisor
Mr Patterson, the van driver
Harry Farthing and Winnie at the pottery
Mr Swallow, the wharfinger
Mr Rumpling, the barge owner
Mr Clutterbuck, the builder
Horace and Cyril, the bricklayers
Mr Gubbins and Mr Sneed, the dustmen

OPPOSITE: Pugh, Pugh, Barney McGrew, Cuthbert, Dibble and Grubb deal with a tricky situation in *Trumpton*.

TRUMPTON RESIDENTS

The hub of activity, or rather inactivity, was at the county town of *Trumpton*.

The Mayor
Philby, the Mayor's driver
Mr Troop, the town clerk
Mr Clamp, the greengrocer
Captain Flack and his merry band of firefighters
Chippy Minton, the carpenter, his wife Dora and
   their son, Nibbs
Mr Antonio, the ice-cream man
Miss Lovelace from the hat shop with her troublesome
   Pekingeses
Mrs Cobbit, the flower seller
Mr Craddock, the park attendant

Mr Robinson, the window cleaner
Mr Munnings, the printer
Mr Platt, the clockmaker
Raggy Dan, Trumpton's answer to Steptoe
Mr Bolt, the Borough Engineer
Nick Fisher, the bill sticker
Walter Harkin, the painter and decorator
Mr Wilkins, the plumber
Mr Wantage, the telephone engineer, and his
   assistant, Fred
The Artist, who appeared just once, to paint a picture
   of the Town Hall for the Mayor's birthday

The *Camberwick Green* and *Chigley* scripts were penned by Murray himself, but for *Trumpton* author Alison Prince (who'd created another *Watch With Mother* offering, *Joe*) was assigned to write the thirteen scripts. She remembers spending many hours in the back bedroom of Freddie Phillips's house in Surrey, laying down the soundtrack with Phillips, who provided all the music for Murray's three series, and Brian Cant, the narrator. 'Someone else would be there with a stopwatch, timing everything, before we finally recorded the entire soundtrack. Often we did three in a day. We had to keep stopping, though, because the house was on the flight path to Heathrow. We had egg boxes stuck over the walls to try and soundproof it, but when a big jet flew overhead, we stopped recording – the whole process wasn't without its problems.'

Other masters of the stop-frame genre equally capable of turning out low-budget creations were Oliver Postgate and Peter Firmin. Upon forming their own production company, Smallfilms, they chalked up a list of successes, such as *Pogles' Wood, Ivor the Engine, Noggin the Nog* and *Bagpuss*, with the latter recently being crowned most popular BBC kids' show ever – not a bad accolade for the saggy, pink-and-white striped cat whose colouring came about by accident.

'I drew a picture of a marmalade cat,' explains Firmin, 'and asked a company in Kent to produce some marmalade-striped material, but a mistake with the chemicals left it pink!'

Bagpuss is, nevertheless, a seventies' programme, while Ivor, the little steam engine, and Noggin, the Viking prince, began life in the fifties.

Postgate and Firmin's first creation for the sixties was *The Pingwings*, namely Mr and Mrs Pingwing, Paul Pingwing and Penny Pingwing, who lived under junk at the back of a barn. The penguin-like creatures appeared in thirty-two episodes shown by Associated Rediffusion during the early sixties, but Postgate and Firmin's first big hit of the decade came in 1964, when they invited us to observe the world of some little woodland folk who lived in a tree – The Pogles.

Pogles' Wood captured my imagination so much as a child that I couldn't walk in the woods without fear of treading on a Pogle, the small, podgy creatures who lived in a tree's roots. From a converted pigsty and disused cowshed near Canterbury, Postgate and Firmin created thirty-two episodes. Initial instalments were shown in the *Clapperboard* children's slot (not to be confused with the ITV series of the seventies, hosted by Chris Kelly) during the summer of 1965, and featured a witch, as Peter Firmin recalls: 'The first six we wrote told the story of how Pippin, the little boy who was a son of the fairies, hatched from a magic bean plant found by Pogle. He was looked after by Pogle and his wife like an adopted son. It was a complete story written by Oliver and ended with the way they got rid of the witch. With the help of the magic bean plant, Mr Pogle tried wishing her away but it always backfired. Eventually, though, he managed to turn her into a 'nothing', a good idea when you're animating films because Oliver crumpled her up and replaced her with a bit of black foil. In a single frame we were able to make the witch disappear into a ball of nothing.'

A year later, when further episodes were commissioned for transmission under the legendary *Watch With Mother* banner, the witch was given the elbow after BBC executives deemed her too frightening for kiddies. Nowadays, she lives in a vase on Oliver Postgate's mantelpiece.

With the Pogles living in a wood, the focus shifted towards the countryside. 'They were in the ideal situation to explore the countryside, to discuss farming, haymaking, road building, all manner of events that take place around us,' says Firmin.

Oliver Postgate remembers the problems associated with creating the woodland series: 'Each programme started with a long country shot, then

AROUND THE WORLD   1960

The year kicked off with the BBC announcing that it wanted to launch a second television channel, although later in the year plans for the introduction of colour television in the UK were to be shelved indefinitely. In May, MPs gave an unopposed second reading to a bill aimed at curbing problems caused by Teddy Boys and during the summer months, the first NHS hearing aids were introduced. By the end of the year, we were waving goodbye to the farthing, as well as national service, which had begun in 1939.

New national service recruits being issued with their kit at the Royal West Kent Depot in Maidstone in 1954.

BASIL BRUSH

Laugh like a hyena? More like a howitzer, really. Basil the posh fox has been laughing outrageously at his own jokes and blasting out his famous 'Boom-boom' catchphrase for over forty years. He first appeared on ITV in September 1962 in the *Small Time* children's slot along with his friends Bert Scampi and Spikey, together known as *The Three Scampis*. The eighteen-inch high fox puppet was made by Peter Firmin, although actor Ivor Owen also had a hand in creating Basil – quite literally. Ivor was the puppeteer who controlled Basil and supplied his distinctive voice.

Basil's television career moved on when he joined the BBC to appear on magician David Nixon's show, *Now for Nixon* in 1967. The following year, the BBC launched *The Basil Brush Show*, featuring Rodney Bewes as Basil's companion in a sketch show with musical numbers from chart-topping acts. Over the years, Basil's companions changed, 'Mr Rodney,' giving way to 'Mr Derek' (Derek Fowlds), 'Mr Roy' (Roy North), 'Mr Howard' (Howard Williams) and 'Mr Billy' (Billy Boyle).

After leaving the BBC in 1980, Basil appeared to have hung up his brush for good by 1986 but was back with a 'Boom-boom' for the first of the Beeb's new sitcom-style *Basil Brush Show*s in 2002.

a close-up of the little noticeboard saying: "Pogles' Wood". Some of the shots featured children – mine or Peter's. We shot outdoors whenever possible, but walking the Pogles in single frame shots across the landscape was like walking under a neon sign thanks to the various fluctuations in light. I got away with it sometimes, but mostly we filmed those sequences inside.

'We had a big table with the landscape backing away from it. Once a week, I went out with secateurs and cut greenery. Sometimes, later in the week, it looked as if autumn had arrived and the leaves would become saggy, so it was vital we had new greenery each week.'

Before the decade was out, Postgate and Firmin would be enjoying a taste of colour television with the first of twenty-six films featuring pink mouse-like creatures living on a distant moon made of cheese. The idea for *The Clangers* (1969-72, although a special one-off episode, 'Vote for Froglet', was shown in 1974 to accompany the General Election) originated from a *Noggin the Nog* 'first reader' book called *Noggin and the Moon Mouse*, in which a large mouse in a duffle coat arrives on the moon in a spaceship fuelled by vinegar and soap flakes.

Postgate explains: 'At the time of developing *The Clangers*, so-called because of the noisy dustbin lids used to protect the entrances into the Clangers' holes, we wanted to focus on space because man was just about to set foot on the moon.' The series was so well received that a NASA official even described it – without a trace of irony – as an attempt to introduce a note of realism to the fantasy of the space race.

The idea of Clangers living under dustbin lids was inspired by one of Postgate's sons: 'He was only two or three at the time, but was talking about a film he was going to make concerning a giant called Edward who lived on the moon. I asked what he ate, and he said, "Tomato soup." I then enquired where he got soup on the moon. He replied, "The moon is full of soup." He continued to explain that you get soup out by unscrewing the volcanoes. So this idea of having soup inside and having an accessible volcano emerged. One has to get a germ of an idea then expand it.'

Inspiration can come from anywhere, and for Michael Bond it was the view he saw looking out his window. One of my stop-frame favourites, *The Herbs*, joined the *Watch With Mother* club in 1968. While Bond provided the stories, esteemed animator Ivor Wood, who later helped bring *Postman Pat* to television, was responsible for creating the puppets who'd made their home in the secret herb garden.

Bond remembers the unexpected phone call which brought the opportunity to pen the series. 'A few days previously, I'd been looking out of the window at my herb garden. I began watching the leaves of parsley blowing in the wind and thought they resembled a lion's mane. Then, Doreen Stephens, Head of Children's Television, phoned asking if I had any ideas suitable for *Watch With Mother*.

'Although extremely busy, I hate turning work down, so outlined an idea where all the characters were named after herbs. She asked for a pilot script and then commissioned thirteen fifteen-minute films.'

Knowing little about herbs, Bond rushed to his local bookshop.

'The way this book described the plants sparked off ideas for the characters and their personalities.' Bond

'I then enquired where he got the soup from. He replied, "The Moon is full of soup." He continued to explain that you get soup by unscrewing the volcanoes.'

explains. 'A good example was belladonna, the ideal name for a witch because it's poisonous.'

But just like Postgate and Firmin's witch a few years earlier, the character was dropped.

Another of Bond's brainwaves which never came to fruition was to open each episode in a kitchen, with an actor adopting the guise of a chef to tell the story over a mixing bowl. 'I thought it would help the plot along and at the same time provide a relatively painless educational element. Somewhere along the line the idea was dropped because the budget for *Watch With Mother* was strictly limited.'

There was a magical quality to Bond's creation, exemplified by the old-fashioned walled garden owned by Lady Rosemary and Sir Basil. Viewers were only allowed in after uttering the magic word, 'Herbidacious', but our allotted time was short. After a brief moment in the company of Parsley, the clownish lion, the 'rather fat, feathery owl called Sage', or Dill, the little dog who was always skittering around desperately trying to chew off his fluffy tail, we were shown the door by Parsley until the following week's visit.

Animator Ivor Wood created many such distinctive characters. With their overgrown heads and slender bodies, his characterizations populated

BELOW: In 1968, you could only visit Parsley the lion's garden if you could say 'Herbidacious.'

several fictitious worlds. He first came to the fore working on *The Magic Roundabout*, which spun on to our screens in 1965. The brainchild of Frenchman Serge Danot has since become a cultural phenomenon, spawning an abundance of merchandise, records, a 1990s' remake narrated by former *Young One*, Nigel Planer (after some lucky soul stumbled across some episodes never seen this side of the English Channel), and, of course, the recent movie.

While working for a Parisian advertising agency in 1963, Danot dreamed up an idea concerning a roundabout operator, some children and a magic garden, which he called *Le Menege Enchante* (*The Enchanted Merry-go-round*). Recruiting the help of Ivor Wood and his wife, Josiane, they burned the midnight oil until their first story was complete, spotlighting the roundabout owner – alias Mr Rusty – who was saddened when the children stopped visiting his roundabout. Suddenly a magic creature, later to be christened Zebedee, entered his life and promised to use enchantment to entice the kids back.

Danot had already created the children, including leading girl, Florence (originally called Margote), but it was Wood who suggested introducing the animals. Arguably the most famous character was Dougal (originally called Pollux), that golden lump of fluff who glided balletically across the ground, even though he had no legs! Adding limbs would have caused additional headaches when it came to the animation, so they followed the old adage, 'simple is best'.

Danot and his team were rewarded for their diligence with an instant hit when French television station ORTF first broadcast the show on 8 October 1964, but launching it on British television was more troublesome. Realizing the market potential of the sugar-loving, long-haired Dougal and Co., ORTF offered it abroad, suggesting it could easily be dubbed into the appropriate language. The Beeb didn't agree and declined the series, stating that it would be too difficult to dub into English while retaining the show's originality. A few months later, though, a change of heart saw Joy Whitby, then producer of *Play School*, champion the cause. In making it suitable for transmission, she had to replace a noisy French soundtrack with something more mellow. She also needed a narrator, but soon realized she already worked with the ideal candidate, the late Eric Thompson (father of actress Emma Thompson). He was working for Whitby on *Play School* and was given examples of the French version to consider. Discarding the storylines and working solely from the pictures, he devised his own stories. Holing himself up in a tiny cottage in Scotland, he wrote a script and was offered the job.

The first screening on British television was at 5.50 p.m. on 18 October 1965, five minutes before the early evening news, exposing it not just to kids, but to parents as well. It was a sure-fire winner from day one, but if the Beeb's executives were unaware of just how popular it had become, they quickly realized when, in 1966, they decided to switch its transmission time back to 4.55 p.m. Fans gave the BBC hierarchy a stern rebuke: even adults swamped the *Junior Points of View* production office with letters of complaint, and within four weeks *The Magic Roundabout* was restored to its normal slot. Production stopped in France in the late sixties but, with hundreds of five-minute films available, the BBC continued its original run until 1977, by which time the show was a worldwide success.

While some programmes were set in a world of fantasy and magic, seducing children's imaginations, others were deliberately rooted in realism, such as *Joe*, an oft-neglected little gem about a dungaree-wearing boy with a basin-style haircut whose parents owned a transport café.

Joe was a different style of children's series using beautifully illustrated flat artwork, such as you would find in a children's book, rather than model figures. The scripts were written by biographer and children's author Alison Prince, and illustrations were supplied by Joan Hickson, the two women having met while out with their babies in a park in Putney,

WHO RODE THE MAGIC ROUNDABOUT?

Do you remember the gang who lived their lives in Serge Danot's little roundabout world? The best known and most frequently seen child was Florence, of course, but there was a rarely seen trio of Rosalie, Basil and Paul too. Other principal characters were guitar-strumming rabbit, Dylan; roundabout owner, Mr Rusty; Zebedee, the self-appointed guardian who always sprung onto the set to announce it was time for bed; Mr MacHenry and his trike; Ermintrude, the cow with a flower in her hair; Brian the Snail and, of course, the fluffy lump called Dougal.

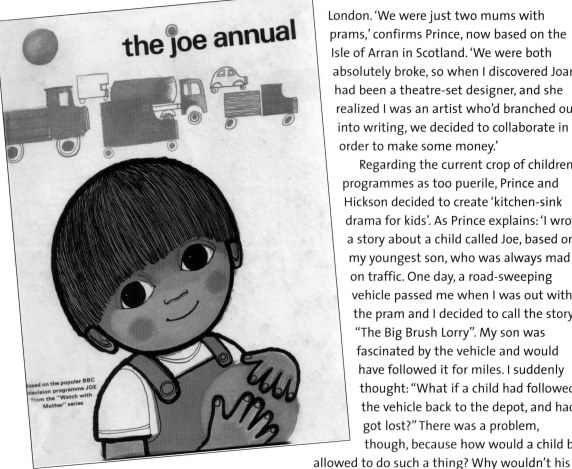

the joe annual

based on the popular BBC television programme JOE from the "Watch with Mother" series

ABOVE: The adventures of *Joe* were hugely popular with children but also caused a great deal of controversy.

London. 'We were just two mums with prams,' confirms Prince, now based on the Isle of Arran in Scotland. 'We were both absolutely broke, so when I discovered Joan had been a theatre-set designer, and she realized I was an artist who'd branched out into writing, we decided to collaborate in order to make some money.'

Regarding the current crop of children's programmes as too puerile, Prince and Hickson decided to create 'kitchen-sink drama for kids'. As Prince explains: 'I wrote a story about a child called Joe, based on my youngest son, who was always mad on traffic. One day, a road-sweeping vehicle passed me when I was out with the pram and I decided to call the story, "The Big Brush Lorry". My son was fascinated by the vehicle and would have followed it for miles. I suddenly thought: "What if a child had followed the vehicle back to the depot, and had got lost?" There was a problem, though, because how would a child be allowed to do such a thing? Why wouldn't his mother do exactly what I did: take his hand and walk safely home?'

Prince found her answer while driving along in her battered car and noticing a transport café with a car park full of large trucks. On the café's doorstep sat a small child. 'I suddenly thought, "That's it! I've cracked it." If the child lives in a transport café, his parents are inside frying chips and dishing out peas, it's quite reasonable that they wouldn't see him wander off.'

Completing her story, Prince passed the text for illustration to Hickson, who based Joe on a friend's son. 'James was just about the right age. He was a gorgeous little chap with this patch of hair, big brown eyes and round face. So I more or less took him as my model.'

They intended to publish the story as a book, before a friend of Hickson's was so enchanted by the material, he suggested making a short film to try to tempt the BBC into commissioning the idea for television. 'In those days there were gaps between programmes and they'd run fillers,' explains Prince. 'A famous one from that period was a scrap of film showing a potter's hands working in clay on a wheel. We thought our tiny bit of film might work as a filler.'

Unfortunately, the friend who made the four-foot scrap of film subsequently went bust, resulting in Prince and Hickson having to buy it back from the official receivers for £30. 'It was a lot of money for us in those broke days,' admits Prince, 'but we managed to get it together and sent the film off to the BBC in the faint hope of recouping the money expended.'

On 2 December 1965, Alison Prince and Joan Hickson met Doreen Stephens, then Head of Family Programmes at the BBC, to discuss *Joe*. Prince supplied sample scripts but, hearing that Stephens was considering *Joe* for *Watch With Mother*, Prince wanted to rework her idea.

She subsequently wrote to Stephens, saying: 'The scripts which I gave you seem in retrospect to have crept into a more senior age group and have not got quite the awful simplicity I want for *Joe* . . . I enclose another story, "Flags", which is deliberately keyed to musical mood-tunes.'

'Flags' became the show's pilot episode and was pre-recorded in Television Centre's Studio E on 17 February 1966. The narrator was none other than Prunella Scales, who'd go on to make her name appearing in classic sixties'

AROUND THE WORLD　　　1961

Kiddies everywhere were reaching for their hankies in January when the long-running radio programme, *Children's Hour*, on air since 1922, was ditched, but there was cause for rejoicing among the adult population when 'The Pill' went on sale. The world stood astonished as Russian Major Yuri Gagarin became the first man in space – much to the Americans' chagrin – when he orbited Earth for 108 minutes. And for those who liked a little flutter, betting shops legally opened their doors for the first time.

sitcom, *The Marriage Lines*, and, a decade later, as Sybil Fawlty in *Fawlty Towers*. Scales completed the recording of the £350 pilot but was later replaced by actor Lee Montague for the commissioned series of thirteen episodes. In a letter to Scales, whose performance was classed as 'delightful', Doreen Stephens explained that it was felt the programme would be 'even better if we added the rough quality of a man's voice as narrator'.

When the series aired in 1966, *Joe* received a warm welcome from many critics, with the *Daily Express*'s Shona Crawford Poole classing it as a 'welcome addition to the viewing menu for tiny tots. It is new. It is different.' *Joe* merchandise became popular and the kiddies' comic, *Pippin*, carried a regular strip – but not everyone was enamoured of the series.

Parents wrote to the BBC drawing attention to the dangers of children playing around parked vehicles. On 10 October 1966, Doreen Stephens replied to one concerned parent, stating: 'There is nothing in this series likely to encourage children to play around in a dangerous way with lorries and cars. We feel the more familiar they are with them, the less likely they are to be tempted to play where they should not. On the other hand we feel that when something is forbidden, it tends to arouse a child's curiosity and may even present a "dare".'

Stephens added that transmitting it in the *Watch With Mother* slot would 'provide a useful opportunity for parents who wish to, to use it as a background for talking to their children on the "whys" and "wherefores" of roadsense.'

Stephens informed Prince of the criticism the series had received. In a letter dated 23 November 1966, she said: 'I think it is right that you should know of the slight criticism we have had on this series so that when we do any future series we can use experience to help us carry as wide a public as possible with us.'

Prince replied a week later, admitting that she anticipated some criticism on the grounds of 'danger and ill-discipline'. She apologised that *Joe* was proving to be a 'troublesome child', but explained that 'if you rule out all undesirable elements there remains little else to write about. After all, most of the classic works for children contain terrifying and tragic situations.'

To begin with the BBC were more than a little hesitant about embarking on a second series of *Joe*, despite Prince and Hickson having already begun their preparations. When Prince raised the matter with Monica Sims, the Head of Children's Programmes, Sims explained the corporation's initial hesitancy was a result of 'some disappointment at the audience's reaction to *Joe*. It is the least popular of the *Watch With Mother* programmes even though half the audience likes it very much indeed.' However, she then broke the good news that discussions had just taken place regarding the *Watch With Mother* schedules for the next five years and a further series was required.

The new series, transmitted in 1971, was shot in colour and saw Joe moving with his parents to the seaside. The little boy's mother was expecting a child and the series focused on his adjustment to life with a baby sister. In a memo to the Controller of the BBC, dated 27 August 1969, Monica Sims explained that the new series would have a 'good deal more pace and variety than the previous series'.

Joan Hickson believes the complaints received by the Beeb probably played a part in the decision to change the setting.

'The BBC were consciously worried about that sort of thing and decided to re-commission a series that had a safer location,' Hickson explains. 'Alison and I thought it awfully silly because at the same time everybody was raving about Noddy and his little car. It was nice to be in colour with the second series, but I never thought it captured the feel of the first. It went a bit middle-class.'

What *Joe* successfully achieved was to offer a realistic, down-to-earth view of the world from a child's perspective, instead of falling within the normal parameters expected of children's programmes. This concept was adopted, albeit to a lesser degree, by *Mary, Mungo and Midge*, which told of the adventures – more usually misadventures – experienced by Mungo, a lugubrious dog, and Midge, a mischievous mouse, when they were let off the leash by Mary, the little girl who owned them.

The first of thirteen episodes was transmitted on BBC in October 1969. The setting was not a fantasy world or rural idyll, but a bustling town full of blocks of flats, in one of which lived Mary, Mungo and Midge. As the programme's narrator pointed out, the trio lived right at the top of an eight-storey block, in the flat with the bright, all-year-blooming flowers in the window box.

John Ryan, who also created *Captain Pugwash*, the rumbustious, overweight pirate who first sailed onto our screens in 1957, designed the characters and settings for *Mary, Mungo and Midge*. Scripts for the series, meanwhile, were supplied by Daphne Jones, a director in the BBC's children's department, who later wrote *On the Farm*, a live-action series screened in 1970.

Ryan explains the rationale behind *Mary, Mungo and Midge*: 'The BBC wanted something realistic and modern, something urban as opposed to cuddly country stories. They also wanted something educational, such as what happens when you post a letter? What happens in hospitals? That

> '**The BBC wanted something realistic and modern, something urban as opposed to cuddly country stories. They also wanted something educational, such as what happens when you post a letter?**'

kind of thing. I saw Mungo as a rather pompous old thing – he was the establishment. Midge was the curiosity bit, so it was the establishment versus curiosity.'

With BBC newsreader Richard Baker narrating and providing voices for Mungo and Midge, it was Isabel Ryan – John's daughter – who brought Mary to life.

Priscilla, John's wife, recalls: 'The BBC spent ages trying to find a voice for the little girl. We listened to some of them and I remember turning to John and saying, "Each one is worse than the last – why don't we try our own daughter?" She was about ten then, and had a very nice, clear speaking voice. We recorded her and sent it off to the BBC without saying who it was. They liked her straight away.'

Isabel was paid £4 for every recording session at the United Motion Pictures in London's Fitzroy Square.

'I'd be handed the script and would sit in the recording studio with Richard Baker and my dad,' she recalls. 'We'd go through it once or twice, and there'd always be a lot of laughing before recording it. It was tremendous fun. Although we giggled a lot, we were always professional. And I remember Mary was quite a solemn little girl, whereas I wasn't, so I had to concentrate on that.'

Isabel Ryan watches the programmes with her daughter, even today: 'She loves them dearly. The quality of the imagery is superb. What's extraordinary for me, looking at them now, is the ability of the faces to have expression, and a series of expressions – even though the technique is very limited. Don't forget, it was all done with flat cardboard cut-outs, levers and dividing pins. If a car drives along the road, it's just being pulled on a lever. I find it amazing to see how specific and graphic those shows are.'

The introduction of colour enabled John Ryan, in his inimitable style, to create vibrant characters and settings but, as Isabel explains, consideration had to be given to viewers who still owned black-and-white television sets. 'My dad had a colour meter, which was a little lens, and we'd look at coloured cardboard to see how it would appear on a black-and-white set.'

Children's programmes in the sixties weren't all about animation: some series, such as *Animal Magic*, introduced their young audience to a host of real creatures that many children had never seen before. When the BBC's Natural History Unit was established in Bristol, presenter Johnny Morris was asked to star in a new weekly show, playing a zookeeper at Bristol Zoo. Morris was no stranger to children's TV. A year earlier, *Hot Chestnut Man*, in which he told his own children's stories from a make-believe street corner in between selling chestnuts from his barrow, had finished after an eight-year run. *Animal Magic* started in 1962 and ran for over twenty years, during which time Morris often risked his own safety in the name of television,

OPPOSITE: Johnny Morris talked to the animals when he played a zoo keeper in *Animal Magic*.

ABOVE: Seatbelt regulations were more relaxed when *Tales of the Riverbank* was filmed.

frequently entering the animals' cages accompanied by an anxious cameraman. Remarking on such scenes, Morris once wrote: 'The more equipment you introduce into an animal's enclosure, the more trouble you heap upon yourself. I have seen a young gorilla simply rip a tripod from a cameraman's grasp and bash him over the head with it. He was not observing rule number one, which is, "Never go into a great ape's enclosure with anything in your hand." It will first be taken from you and then you'll get it back with a vengeance.'

Animal Magic came to an end in the early eighties, a sad occasion for Johnny Morris.

'It was hated by the scientific section of the BBC's Natural History Unit because it was anthropomorphic – that is, it treated animals like humans,' he told me. 'It had a disappointing end, especially as the public loved it. Gradually, the faces responsible for *Animal Magic* were replaced by people who seemed to know little about animals. All they were interested in was making sensational programmes.'

Morris's experience of working with animals on a Wiltshire farm on which there were 600 cows and 2,000 pigs made him a perfect choice for playing *Animal Magic*'s zookeeper. He once said: 'Sadly, I don't think it would be possible to make a programme like that today, with all the regulations. It was far more relaxed in my day. I'd been in the job ten years before the BBC discovered I wasn't insured!' The stories fitted round the animals. 'They did what they liked and I created a story around what they were doing. It worked well.'

Working with animals can be fraught with problems, as David Ellison – who created *Tales of the Riverbank* with his Canadian partner, Paul Sutherland – acknowledges. While employed by the BBC, he was transferred to Canada to assist the launch of the Canadian Broadcasting

Corporation (CBC). During the four years spent across the Atlantic, he worked for a French producer who was making a children's series with various animals, including goats, spider monkeys, pigs and chickens. Ellison says: 'It was chaos in the studio, there was no control at all.'

The series failed to impress but gave Ellison an idea. 'I started thinking about using animals for children's television, but small animals that were "handleable". The goats had messed up sets while the spider monkey had disappeared high up into the studio – we couldn't get him down for weeks. It was a total disaster. But if you use smaller animals, like hamsters and guinea pigs, you don't get the problems.'

When Ellison left the CBC he hired a cameraman he'd used while based in the news department, filmed a pilot episode, called it *Tales of the Riverbank* and jumped on a plane for England. Hoping to sell the programme to the BBC, he phoned Owen Reed, Head of Children's Television, and – to his amazement – got an appointment.

'We had a screening in one of the viewing theatres at Ealing, which the BBC had just bought,' says Ellison. 'After the film finished, Reed sat staring at the screen, in silence.'

He eventually looked at Ellison, confirmed he liked the film and once his deputy, Ursula Eason, had also given the thumbs up, a contract for thirteen episodes was issued. Ellison returned to Toronto and set to work with Sutherland, who'd decided to quit his job with CBC. Riverbank Productions was established and operated from the middle of Toronto.

The enchanting televisual world that Ellison and Sutherland created saw Hammy Hamster, Roderick Rat and their friends pootling along in a minuscule motorboat and undertaking daily chores at their riverside homes. Adopting some catchy Hungarian folk music, played by a Canadian folk guitarist, as the theme tune, the show was narrated by Johnny Morris. British children made their first visit to the riverbank in July 1960, and they'd be returning on a regular basis for years to come.

It's estimated that one hundred hamsters were employed in the central role of Hammy; once pensioned off, they were adopted by friends of the production crew. Writing in the *Radio Times* in 1960, Ellison explained that 'all the animals have stand-ins, and no performer is asked to work more than ten minutes at a time. In fact, the weasel refuses to move after only five minutes of work on stage!'

Approximately 12,000 feet of film was shot for each 500-foot instalment, but surely it couldn't have been easy turning untrained animals into film stars? Not so, says Ellison: 'It wasn't as difficult as you think. They were controlled by noise and movement off-screen, and they reacted very well to having cold water on their nose. If we wanted an animal to make a quick movement, say, to the left, we'd make a

'After the film finished, Reed sat staring at the screen, in silence.'

'When Hammy was in the aeroplane he seemed to be frightened.'

loud noise, such as clapping hands or blowing a whistle, on the right. And if you wanted them to move slowly to the left, then we'd put something they liked on the left. If you analyze the programme you'll see that the animals aren't actually doing very much, it's the props that are doing all the work. Take the guinea pig: when he's flying his plane, all he's doing is sitting in the cockpit, it's the plane that's doing all the stunts and making the noises.'

Unfortunately, seeing an animal apparently taking to the skies was too much for a ten-year-old girl from Bristol. Writing to the Beeb, she complained: 'I was unhappy watching this as it seemed to be cruel to the animals. When Hammy was in the aeroplane he seemed to be frightened. He nearly fell on the propellers as they were going round and tried to get out as the plane was flying.'

During the life of the programme, the BBC continued to receive occasional letters from worried viewers – perhaps to be expected, considering the young audience's affinity with the fluffy balls of fur performing on screen. In an attempt to pre-empt further anxieties being expressed to the BBC, Peggy Miller, then at the Beeb's Children's Department, wrote to Ellison in June 1962, regarding her concerns after watching the latest batch of films supplied by Riverbank Productions.

She referred to two instalments in which the hamsters were seen swimming, explaining: 'My first reaction to this was that we would have a lot of children throwing their pet hamsters into the bath ... This may seem a little far-fetched to you, but I assure you from past experience that it is not.'

An exasperated Ellison fired back a quick response, explaining that all the shooting was conducted under the supervision of the Toronto Humane Society, which hadn't objected to the said sequence at all. Ellison pointed out that one member of the Society had even commented that it would at least rid the creature of any fleas crawling around in its fur.

At times, the BBC were oversensitive, blowing matters out of proportion, and as Owen Reed, Head of Children's Television, wrote in April 1963, in response to a letter from a parent: '... animal stories, like grown-up plays, must have their predicaments and adventures. Great care is taken in making these little films, but it is difficult to make absolutely sure that children won't conclude that a hamster actor in a tense situation is actually a terrified animal. If they were, of course, they'd simply run away!'

Tales of the Riverbank was a great success, and not just in Britain. It was shown in over fifty countries, including China and Russia, where it was honoured at the Moscow Film Awards. A second season was made by Ellison, by then living on the Isle of Wight, for ATV in the early 1970s.

Whereas the first season had been made beside a stream running through a Toronto park, these colour instalments were filmed in Ellison's studio near Ryde. The adventures, which took around four weeks to film and edit, continue to entertain kids around the globe today.

Another major player in the world of children's television was Roberta Leigh, who first tasted success in the late 1950s, when Associated Rediffusion screened *The Adventures of Twizzle*, an idea she conceived after making up a story for her son. Leigh devised the idea for the series after a dinner guest gave her not only a bottle of champagne but a silver swizzle stick, too. 'When I asked what it was, he told me it was for getting bubbles out of champagne. I thought it was a ridiculous idea and said that as far as I was concerned it was a twizzle stick because it goes around and around; as I said it, I got the idea for *Twizzle*.'

Her next hit, *Torchy the Battery Boy*, was bought by ABC, who broadcast in the midlands and north of England, and who commissioned two series of twenty-six episodes. Her first new project for the sixties was *Sara and Hoppity* for Associated Rediffusion which, like *Twizzle* and *Torchy*, has since become a cult series. The first of fifty-two episodes of *Sara and Hoppity*, for which Leigh was paid £700, was transmitted in February 1962. It told the story of a little girl, Sara Brown, and her clockwork doll who, with one

BELOW: A toy hospital was the setting for Roberta Leigh's *Sara and Hoppity* in 1962.

leg shorter than the other, was called Hoppity. The show was based on a series of books written by Leigh in which Sara's parents ran a hospital for toys. Hoppity was a goblin toy and occasionally a bad influence, getting Sara into mischief.

The series quickly became popular with children, particularly young girls, but not everyone at Associated Rediffusion was as keen.

After Leigh submitted her first three films, Joan Elman, a member of the production team, wrote to John Rhodes, then Head of Children's Programmes Department, in August 1961, detailing her objections.

Regarding the first episode, 'Sara and Hoppity', she said: 'There is a dangerous use of scissors cutting off hair which could easily be imitated with dangerous results. The illustrated theme song on the lines, "I hate spinach, vegetables, won't eat my bread and butter, feed the milk to the cat and make dirty marks on the door," does nothing but suggest a bad example to children. The detail of a child throwing poached egg and spinach on to the floor is not a proper subject for *Small Time* [their slot for the under-fives] viewers.'

ABOVE: *Hatty Town* became an animated series in 1971 but began life in 1967 as a series of stories narrated with still images on screen.

It was felt such antics might influence children to misbehave, something Roberta Leigh dismisses, pointing out that Sara always got her comeuppance in the end. Ultimately, alterations were made to some of the scripts, but it didn't affect the show's appeal. Sadly, *Sara and Hoppity* is never seen today, denying children the chance to enjoy this little gem. It was originally shown under ITV's *Small Time* banner, a 15-minute segment running between 1955 and 1966, before it was replaced by *Playtime* and, later, *Hullaballoo*. Other shows filling that fifteen minutes included *Musical Box*, *Pippy's Party*, *All at Sea*, *The Scampis* (introducing us to Basil Brush and his pals, Bert Scampi and Spikey, in 1962) and *Hatty Town*.

Although people remember the animated series of *Hatty Town*, originally shown by Thames Television between 1971 and 1972, it did, in fact, begin its screen life in 1967 as part of ITV's *Small Time*. With no animation, each programme was simply a series of illustrations on screen with narration by the man of many voices, Peter Hawkins, who provided voices for so many children's characters, including those on *The Flowerpot Men*. The pictures were by John McLusky.

Later, the series would become an animated show, with animator Ivor Wood helping to bring alive *Hatty Town*'s population, consisting of a collection of talking hats, each with limbs and faces, who lived in oversized hatboxes. Characters included Bobby the Policeman's Helmet and Posty the Postman's Hat, but the storylines usually centred on Sancho and a donkey called Carrots who were adept at solving problems and mysteries for fellow members of the community.

Creator Keith Chatfield recalls how he conceived the idea for *Hatty Town*: 'I wrote the story to keep my son, who's now forty, entertained when he was about five. I was working for the Express Dairy Company in London, and had been at a very important meeting. But it had been so boring, I'd doodled all over the blotting paper in front of me. At the end of the meeting, I took the paper with me because I didn't want anyone else to find it.

'I put it in my pocket and it wasn't until weeks later, while clearing out my pockets, that I found the paper. My son asked what it was and, jokingly, I pointed to the doodles of large hats with big, bulging eyes, and said: "This is very important." Having said that to a five-year-old I had to make it important and started some pictures and storylines.'

A friend of Chatfield's got to hear of his stories and offered them to the BBC before finally selling the concept to Associated Rediffusion. When the first programme was aired in 1967, it was an excited Keith Chatfield who sat down with his family to watch.

'I can't explain how it felt to switch the television on and see a programme by me,' says Chatfield. 'But, in a way, I was disappointed when I saw it because I had assumed they would simply copy the amateurish illustrations which I had done. It gave me an incentive to carry on writing, which I did alongside a career in teaching. Thanks to the royalties from *Hatty Town*, I took a year out to gain a teaching diploma at Reading University and taught in primary schools for twenty years. Having given up teaching, I've since visited about 600 schools giving writing workshops.'

Hatty Town changed Chatfield's life and with a proven track record, he went on to create another children's series, *Issi Noho*, about a loveable panda, which entertained kids in the seventies.

One of the biggest rivalries in children's television was between *Blue Peter* and *Magpie*. The BBC's *Blue Peter*, which began in October 1958, introduced kids to a world of sticky-backed plastic, but had already reached adolescence when Thames Television's *Magpie* flew into the television schedules a decade later.

'I can't explain how it felt to switch the television on and see a programme by me.'

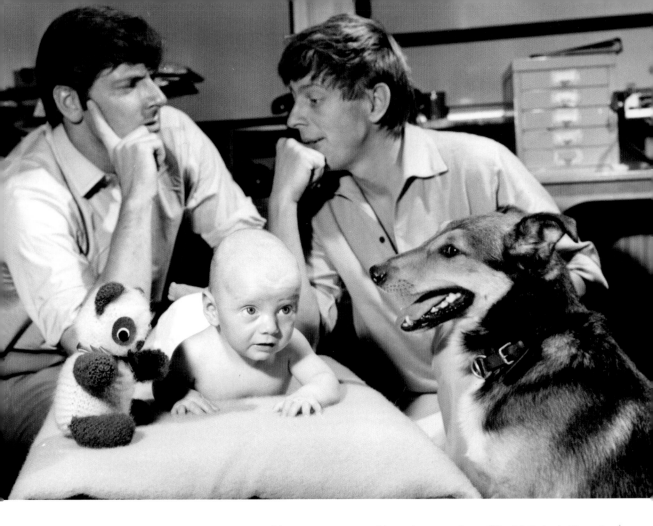

ABOVE: Petra keeps baby Daniel Simon Scott on his best behaviour as Purves and Noakes decide how best to handle their trickiest *Blue Peter* assignment.

Viewed by many as a working-class version of its BBC rival, *Magpie* desperately wanted to be hip, with its opening credits and catchy 'one for sorrow, two for joy' theme tune. Output was soon increased to two instalments a week as the show's original line-up of presenters – Susan Stranks, Tony Bastable and former Radio 1 DJ, Pete Brady – got into their stride. Its BBC rival exuded middle-class cosiness, but *Magpie* boasted a grittier nature. While followers of *Blue Peter* were asked to donate old books, milk-bottle tops and other discarded items towards worthy causes, there was no messing about on *Magpie*, with viewers being cajoled into breaking open their piggy banks.

Initially a husband-and-wife presenting team was considered for *Magpie*, as Susan Stranks explains: 'My late husband, Robin Ray, had been working at Thames Television on a children's music show, *Sounds Exciting*, with a researcher called Sue Turner. A little later, Sue joined a team responsible for assembling a magazine show in the style of *Blue Peter*. They'd seen a programme in Scandinavia hosted by a husband-and-wife team, so Sue asked Robin if we'd like to do it. Robin was involved in something else so couldn't, but I said I'd love to. I'd been largely acting until then and wanted to do some presenting. So when they auditioned they decided to drop the husband-and-wife idea and go for two guys and a girl, and I was lucky enough to get the job. It was called *Magpie* because "mag" represented the fact it was a magazine show and "pie" for the surprise element – so, a magazine full of surprises.'

Each instalment of *Magpie* was unscripted, testing the skill and nerve of its presenters. Although everyone was briefed on the items to be discussed, presenters were given carte blanche to say what they wanted. Over at the Beeb, meanwhile, *Blue Peter* presenters used scripts, which caused its own pressures. Peter Purves, already a familiar face on television before joining the programme, thanks to a stint playing one of *Doctor Who*'s companions, recalls: 'We didn't use autocue in those days, so were given scripts and had to learn them. It was hard work.'

When offered the chance to replace original *Blue Peter* presenter Christopher Trace in 1967, Purves was out of work, but he wasn't sure it was the right move. Initially, he felt that it 'didn't seem like an acting job' but such concerns were soon dispelled and he became one of the programme's stalwarts.

Blue Peter had started off as a seven-part trial in October 1958, fronted by Christopher Trace and Leila Williams, a former Miss Great Britain. Regular visitors to the studio included a host of unpredictable animals. During Purves's time on the show, the animal guests included a baby elephant called Lulu. They say that elephants never forget, but no one will ever forget Lulu – especially not Peter Purves.

Before the *Blue Peter* team jetted off to Sri Lanka on one of their many assignments, viewers were introduced to Lulu, who'd been taught – or so everyone thought – to comply with her keeper's instructions, which were generally accompanied by a quick whack from the heavy stick he carried. Trouble was on the cards, though, as soon as editor Biddy Baxter asked the keeper to discard the stick – after all, the team didn't want to upset any of the delicate blooms tuning in! With no stick to worry about, the elephant grabbed the moment to get her own back for all those bumps on the head and proceeded to embarrass her keeper. As if tearing around the studio wasn't enough, Lulu started doing her business all over the floor and had the temerity to drag her keeper through the mess.

'The keeper tried to get the elephant out of the studio, but failed miserably and the elephant returned,' recalls Purves with a smile. 'It liked us, you see, because we had water and buns, which were much more fun. It was a total shambles but extremely funny. I spent most of the time on air laughing my head off.'

Magpie had to endure its share of animal embarrassments, too, such as the adorable little pony who became something of a regular at the Teddington Studios, the crew and presenters nicknaming him the 'pony

'... before I could climb out of the basket the balloon – filled with hydrogen – exploded dramatically.'

with five legs', because he always became aroused upon entering the studios. And, of course, there was a steady supply of other creatures pooping everywhere. Susan Stranks, who remained with the show until 1974, remembers a cute baby seal being brought into the studio. 'It started to pee all over the place. They do an awful lot of pee, but it also smells appalling – it's like cod liver oil. It was terrible.'

One of *Blue Peter*'s most popular presenters was John 'Action Man' Noakes, who'd do anything in the line of duty, including scaling Nelson's Column, or diving from a plane to become the first British civilian to undertake a 25,000-foot free-fall parachute descent. Not wanting to be outdone, *Magpie* presenters endured their fair share of courageous feats. While recording footage for her first filmed feature, Susan Stranks took part in a balloon race in Sussex, a day she remembers for all the wrong reasons.

'We were filming throughout the flight and landed safely. I was last out, but before I could climb out of the basket, the balloon – filled with hydrogen – exploded dramatically. I was knocked out for a few seconds by the sound box strapped to me, and when I came round I bolted behind a hedge. I still have a scar today. Quite literally, that was my baptism of fire.'

While *Blue Peter*'s extraordinary stamina means the programme is still going strong after nearly fifty years, *Magpie* fluttered its wings for the last time in 1980. Its demise was regretted by many. Mick Robertson, who joined the *Magpie* team in 1972, says: '*Blue Peter* has been a wonderful example of how a television programme can grow and adapt to the age it's in. There's always a sense that it's a little old-fashioned but, in actual fact, it's managed to keep abreast of the times pretty successfully. As for *Magpie*, at the time controllers at ITV thought the show was played out. They might have been right but I think that brands are valuable and difficult to acquire. Once you've got one you throw it away at your peril.'

Other programmes that relied, largely, on human beings to entertain the children, instead of puppets or cartoon characters, included *Play School* and *Jackanory*. One of *Play School*'s original presenters was Brian Cant, who'll forever be remembered for the eighteen years he spent entertaining pre-school kids. Now in his seventies, he'll never forget his audition for *Play School*. 'I met the producer in an office at the BBC, and after chatting for a while she kicked a box out from under the table and said, "Get in there and row out to sea." So I did an ad-lib journey on water, caught a pretend boot on my fishing rod, and after making up some more rubbish, rowed back in, climbed up the table leg and back into my seat. I think the producer was suitably impressed because she asked me to go away and write a script for a film test. I was working on *No Hiding Place*, a police drama, for Rediffusion at the time, and had to dash up one lunchtime to audition. Luckily, I got the job and in 1964 joined the team. I stayed eighteen years and had a wonderful time, but it's funny to think the original contract was only for three months.'

Inevitably, things went wrong, but as the show was recorded rather than being broadcast live, they had the chance to paper over the cracks. Cant recalls: 'Once this guy brought an eagle into the studio, assuring us that it didn't need to be tethered. It sat on his arm until something frightened it and it flew up and crashed into the lights before relieving itself. All this muck was falling down and we ended up having to clear the studio.'

One of the show's trademarks, in addition to the mysterious round, square and arched windows through which the viewers were invited to

BELOW: Brian Cant and Carole Ward with two animal friends on *Play School* in 1964.

look in order to enjoy a sequence of film, were the toys on the programme – Humpty, Big and Little Ted, Jemima and Hamble. 'I think the only one we had to replace in all the time we did the show was Big Ted, who was stolen,' says Cant. 'He suddenly disappeared. Eric Morecambe was rehearsing in another studio and came in for a chat. He was mortified when he heard about Ted.'

A pilot of *Play School*, with its 'Here's a house – Here's a door – And windows, one, two, three, four! Ready to knock – Turn the lock – It's *Play School!*' chant over the opening credits was transmitted on 31 March 1964. Promoted as a 'programme for children at home, most of whom are unable to go to nursery school', encouraging children to 'enjoy discovering for themselves their own latent mental and physical abilities through play – learning with fun', it became the first programme transmitted on BBC2. The show was broadcast Monday to Friday between 11.00 and 11.30 a.m., with each day's broadcast carrying a particular emphasis: Mondays being 'Useful Box Day'; Tuesdays 'Dressing Up Day'; Wednesdays 'Pets and Living Things Day'; Thursdays 'Imagination Day'; and Fridays 'Science Day'.

It didn't take long for the series to establish itself and it was soon selling abroad to Italy, Switzerland and Australia, among others. Primary schools up and down the country showed the programme to their reception classes, and it received positive reviews in the national press. In 1966, the *Sunday Times* classed it as the 'best of all programmes for the under-fives' because, the reporter felt, it took the same approach as nursery school by letting children experience the everyday world, 'catching their interest and channelling their enthusiasm without actually directing them . . . it never falls into the trap of talking down or being arch.'

Anna Home, who became BBC's Head of Children's Programmes in 1986, worked on *Play School* as a research assistant and concurs with the journalists' reactions from that time. 'The presenters were not authoritarian, it was all very anti-authority. It was meant to be fun, not grown-ups telling you what to do.'

The then editor of *Play School*, Joy Whitby, said: 'Small children are much tougher-minded than many parents suppose . . . We try and encourage them to be creative and think for themselves . . . It isn't a case of "now do what I do", but rather "do what you want to do in your own particular way".'

When launched, the original aim was to create a repertory company of presenters, young men and women drawn from the acting and teaching professions, and over the years the long list of presenters included Emma Thompson's parents, Phyllida Law and Eric Thompson, Johnny Ball, Floella Benjamin, Julie Stevens, Derek Griffiths, Valerie Pitts, Carole Ward, Paul Danquah and Rick Jones, who went on to front *Fingerbobs*.

Later repeated on BBC1, before eventually transferring to One, the show

ABOVE: Julie Stevens in 1964 on *Play School* with rag doll Jemima and Humpty.

became an institution in the world of children's television, as did *Jackanory* which, as Anna Home explains, grew out of *Play School*. 'We had a story-telling slot in *Play School*. It was felt that it would be a good idea to do longer stories for a slightly older audience, which is how *Jackanory* was born.'

Aimed at seven- to twelve-year-olds, *Jackanory* eventually became a show on which stars clamoured to appear. Over the years, actors and well-known personalities read the weekly stories, including Margaret Rutherford, James Robertson Justice, Kenneth Williams, Judi Dench, George Cole, Jon Pertwee and Jane Asher. But it was actor Lee Montague who turned the first pages when he read a series of short stories on 13 December 1965. Anna Home explains how the style of the show evolved: 'At the beginning, when nobody knew about it, people weren't terribly interested, but when the acting profession realized it was exposure for fifteen minutes, five days a week, they got much more excited about it. And in the early days, there were a lot of "real" people, as opposed to actors, including a guy called Bob Roberts, who sailed barges around the

'I got a lot of letters from girls wanting to know where I bought my clothes. Another girl wrote asking why I wore a bra.'

east coast, telling his own story. Several other people did that, although it faded out latterly and became mainly actors.'

A ground-breaking series which began life in 1964 was *Vision On*. Geared towards deaf children, it became a beacon of social inclusion and ran until 1977, making household names of, among others, presenters Pat Keysell and Tony Hart. Keysell was part of the production team on *For Deaf Children*, the show it superseded. In her desire to cater for deaf children among the audiences watching children's television, Ursula Eason, the long-standing Deputy Head of Children's Programmes, launched the monthly show, *For Deaf Children*, in 1952. The *Radio Times* reported that the show 'makes capital of the heightened visual awareness of most deaf children. Sport, cartoons, handicrafts, competitions, quizzes, variety turns, and plays have all been successfully presented in a series which is helping break down the barrier of loneliness for thousands of handicapped children.'

By 1964, however, the format was in need of an overhaul and *Vision On* emerged, eventually going on to sell around the world. Pat Keysell, a former actress, joined the BBC as a production secretary, initially working for Ursula Eason. Knowing of Keysell's acting background, Eason offered her the chance to present *Vision On*.

Keysell was hugely enthusiastic about the new show. 'The thing about *For Deaf Children* was that it pointed the finger and said: "You are deaf children, you are different." It was also a very ponderous programme. The premise behind *Vision On* was that it would become a programme for all children but, because it was so visual, it would appeal to deaf children, too.'

For the first year, Keysell – who also worked as a visiting mime teacher in schools for the deaf in London – presented *Vision On* alone until joined by artist Tony Hart. Transmitted weekly from BBC Bristol, this innovative programme, with its quirky Tony Hart-drawn logo, was chiefly art-based and one of its most popular segments was 'The Gallery', which each week exhibited a tiny sample of the thousands of children's paintings and drawings that deluged the Beeb's production office.

As well as paintings, the presenters received bags of fan mail, too. 'People asked the strangest things,' recalls Keysell, who stayed with the show until its demise in 1977, and now runs Compass Community Arts in Eastbourne. 'I got lots of letters from girls wanting to know where I bought my clothes. Another girl wrote asking why I wore a bra. Apparently she'd been told at school that it was best not to because they weakened the muscles. I replied saying I was told the opposite in my day at school and that it was good to have the support. I also mentioned that Marilyn Monroe slept in her bra, so there must be something in it!'

For the scientifically-minded kids around, or those too inquisitive for their own good, Southern Television's long-running series, *How!*, which was networked around the country, was essential viewing. A *Tomorrow's World* for youngsters, *How!* ran between 1966 and 1981, boasting a line-up of Fred Dinenage, Bunty James (later replaced by Marian Davies), Jack Hargreaves and Jon Miller. Each week, the team provided answers to all those unfathomable mysteries niggling at the viewers' young minds – and, to be honest, many adult minds, too.

Fred Dinenage, who was twenty-three when the series began, explains the show's origins: 'It was devised by Jack Hargreaves, a great natural broadcaster in his own right, who'd enjoyed a long-running series called *Out of Town*, which was networked and sold around the world. He was also Deputy Controller of Programmes at Southern TV for many years. He originally envisaged *How!* as a programme for adults, so the first programme we made was put out at 10.30 in the evening.'

Hargreaves soon realized, though, that it appealed to children, too, so

BELOW: *Vison On* regulars Pat Keysell, Ben Benison, Tony Hart and Wilfred Makepeace Lunn, pose with Grog, the *Vision On* logo.

when a series was commissioned it was given the 5.15 p.m. slot, just before the early evening news.

Such was the show's popularity, the team made up to thirty-nine instalments a year, with kids adopting the trademark *How!* hand signal.

'Jack Hargreaves concentrated on general knowledge items,' recalls Dinenage. 'Jon Miller's great interest in life was explosions, and he was particularly good at them, so we had lots in the studio. Frequently the fire alarms were set off and the local fire brigade would come round. The wonderful Bunty James, now living in the far north of Scotland, used to do the make-and-do and cookery items, whereas my role was really to cock things up!

'I remember we'd completed the first two programmes, which I'd messed up horribly, and Jack would never do retakes. How it happened was how it went out, that's what he liked. I started realizing that *How!* was going to be a good show and told myself that I must really make an effort. For the next two weeks, my work was perfect, but Jack took me to one side and said: "Look, we didn't hire you to do this, your job is to make us laugh, so make as many cock-ups as you like." That came easy to me!'

The show, in its original format, ran until Southern Television lost its franchise in 1981, but it has since been revived as *How2*, with Fred Dinenage still presenting the programme. He has nothing but happy memories of those days with Jack and the team, but readily admits that not everything went to plan, like the time he tried explaining how golf balls were painted.

'To demonstrate the impossibility of doing it by hand, I had a golf ball, a pair of large tweezers and a can of white spray paint. In those days, Bunty and I sat on the back row, slightly above Jon and Jack and, unfortunately for me and Jon Miller, as I pressed the can of white paint, the nozzle stuck and a huge jet shot out, catching Jon in the back of the head. He couldn't get the paint off, so for several weeks afterwards all I could see was this white blob in front of me, which was the back of Jon Miller's head. Working on the show was heaven because I was being paid to do something which was great fun.'

The sixties also saw imports becoming increasingly prevalent. Offerings from around the globe were fighting their way into the TV schedules, including *Skippy*, the bush kangaroo, one of Australia's most famous exports. Set in Waratah National Park, the show, which ran to nearly 100 episodes between 1967 and 1969, told the story of a kangaroo who, having been saved from certain death by the Chief Ranger's son, Sonny, shows his gratitude – if that's possible for a kangaroo – by alerting the boy to potential dangers.

It quickly became a worldwide hit and marked the screen debut for a young English-born actress. Playing Clarissa Merrick was Liza Goddard, who's best remembered for playing Philippa Vale in the Jersey-based detective series, *Bergerac*, and April Winter in the final series of *The Brothers*. Goddard recalls: 'When I was fifteen, my father, who worked for the BBC, was invited to become Head of Drama for the Australian Broadcasting Corporation. The whole family moved and that's where, aged seventeen, I began acting. I started off in *Skippy*.

'We did ninety-two episodes in two years, which was like working in a factory, but it became a huge hit. Over the years we used about twenty Skippys, partly because they kept running off into the bush! We also had a bad-tempered emu who needed half a bottle of scotch before he was safe to work with. Koalas were tame in comparison!'

Another foreign import featuring live animals was American-produced series *Daktari*, a successful spin-off from MGM's 1965 film, *Clarence the Cross-Eyed Lion*. Filmed between 1966 and 1969, *Daktari*, a Swahili word for 'doctor', centred on day-to-day life at Wameru Study Centre for Animal Behaviour in East Africa. Location shooting wasn't in Africa, but in a wild-animal park in California, yet that didn't diminish the feeling of adventure in the series. Vet Dr Marsh Tracy was assisted by his daughter, Paula, but the show's two most memorable characters were Judy, the mischievous chimp and, of course,

'Over the years we used about twenty Skippys, partly because they kept running off into the bush!'

cross-eyed Clarence the lion. Many lion cubs are born temporarily cross-eyed, but in Clarence's case the problem didn't rectify itself.

Believe it or not, an eye specialist from the University of California prescribed glasses for the lion, but not surprisingly Clarence didn't take too kindly to the idea. The animal possessed highly sensitive eyes, ears and nose, causing major headaches for the directors because the slightest distraction would rouse his interest.

Other offerings during the sixties included *Tom Tom*, *Chippy*, *Orlando*, *Pinky and Perky*, *Tich and Quakers,* and who can forget *Hector's House*, first shown on BBC1 in 1968? A French production, titled *La Maison de Tou Tou*, it was set in a sunny back garden where Zaza, a very practical, level-headed cat, and Kiki, a sensitive, shy frog, spent much of their time playing tricks on poor old Hector, a floppy-eared, clumsy dog. And what about *Bonehead*, which ran to three series between 1960 and 1962? This light-hearted comedy serial on Saturday afternoons spotlighted the criminal capers of Bonehead, Boss and Happy, played by Colin Douglas, Paul Whitsun-Jones and Douglas Blackwell.

The BBC must have considered themselves rather innovative when they brought *Zokko!* to the screen in 1968, the first of two series featuring an animated pinball table linking stories and cartoons, such as the sci-fi strip cartoon serial, *Skayn*, about a heroic astronaut. But the viewers remained undecided about the show. When the BBC's Audience Research Department completed one of its reports in February 1969, it stated: 'There was very nearly as much criticism as there was praise for pinball table and robot devices used for the arrangement and linkage of items, but, on balance, their originality was said to have given *Zokko!* an unusual touch.'

For younger children, meanwhile, 1967 saw *Bizzy Lizzy* joining the *Watch With Mother* club. *Bizzy Lizzy* had first appeared in the earlier *Picture Book* series, presented by Patricia Driscoll and later Vera McKechnie. Although less successful than other output from Freda Lingstrom (who brought us *Andy Pandy* and other classics), it was nevertheless a charming series about a little girl with a flower on her dress who, by virtue of putting her hand on the flower, was granted a daily supply of wishes.

Associated Rediffusion offered us two series of *Badger's Bend* during 1963 and 1964, and three years later produced the popular show containing a plethora of sketches and skits, *Do Not Adjust Your Set*. With a team comprising Eric Idle, Terry Jones, Michael Palin, Denise Coffey and an inexperienced actor called David Jason, it became a ratings winner but in 1969, after two series spread over two years, the set was switched off. It wasn't long before Idle, Jones and Palin were back on our screens, though, this time teaming up with John Cleese and Graham Chapman for the hilarious *Monty Python's Flying Circus*.

Other offerings from Rediffusion included *Muskit and Dido* and shows such as 1963's *Magic Paint Box*, with John Mills (no, not *the* John Mills) and Whiffles having fun with paints; *Music Fairy*, with Sheila Mossman telling stories with puppets Music Fairy and Murky; *Picture the Word*, created by Roberta Leigh and featuring Tikki the Toucan; *Squiffy and Vic*, concerning two red squirrels' adventures in Oak Apple Valley; *Story Book*, which was first introduced by Oliver Postgate; and *Play Time*, presented by Gwyneth Surdivell and Jennifer Naden, who were having fun in their magic park.

BELOW: Garry Pankhurst, as 'Sonny Hammond', becomes embroiled in another adventure with *Skippy*.

THE LAUNCH OF BBC2

Monday, 20 April 1964 is a date indelibly etched in the history of television, although, sadly, perhaps not for the right reasons. It was supposed to be launch day for BBC2, which was intended to meet programming needs not addressed by BBC1 or ITV, but a power strike put paid to the grand launch. A day later, with a candle flickering in a dimly-lit studio (a tongue-in-cheek acknowledgement of the delayed launch) the evening's viewing got under way. The station had, however, kicked off earlier on Tuesday, 21 April thanks to the first instalment of *Play School*, which had a working title of *Home School*, at 11.00 a.m.

If you've ever wondered what televisual delights BBC2 executives had in store for that fateful opening night on 20 April, the *Radio Times* reported:

7.20 *Line-Up* (for Opening Night with John Stone and Denis Tuohy and the latest news)

7.30 *The Alberts' Channel Too* (direct from the Alberts' Television Centre in the heart of London with The Alberts, also appearing are Ivor Cutler of Y'hup O.M.P., Professor Bruce Lacey, John Snagge, Sheree Winton, Benito Mussolini, Major John Glenn, Adolf Hitler, David Jacobs, Birma the Elephant and other celebrities)

8.00 *Kiss Me, Kate* (starring Patricia Morison, Howard Keel, Millicent Martin, Reginald Beckwith and Irving Davies)

9.35 *Arkady Raikin* (the Soviet Union's leading comedian with the Leningrad Miniature Theatre Company)

10.20 *Off with a Bang* (a Grand Fireworks Display to celebrate the opening of BBC2 from beside the seaside – the famous pier at Southend. Lighting the blue paper and stepping well back is Brian Johnston)

10.35 *Newsroom*

11.00 *Closedown* (and a look at tomorrow)

The publicity campaign leading up to the launch of the new channel had featured mascots Hullabaloo and Custard, an adult kangaroo and her baby, the idea being that the baby, representing the newborn BBC2, would emerge from the older kangaroo, symbolizing BBC1.

BBC2 was to be introduced in London and south-east England before being rolled out across the rest of the country, but not everyone was happy with the thought of having more television channels to watch. The idea that more TV would produce a nation of couch potatoes slumped in front of the box all night was being tossed around even then. Kenneth Adam, the BBC Director of Television, confirmed in the *Radio Times* in April 1964 that some religious and social 'leaders' had remarked that a new channel means 'more "vegetating" in front of the set. We shall become even more of a passive, peering people.' Adam stated that 'BBC2 is not an invitation to watch more, to become a television addict,' adding that the station's aim was to 'give people more of what they really like, and some of what, so far, they have not had from television.'

Pointing out that it wasn't anyone's intention to undermine or weaken BBC1 or its commercial rivals, Adam hoped that by the winter of 1966-7, the signal would be beaming into the homes of two-thirds of the population, some 35 million people. Adam's forecasts were a little wayward because, as confirmed by Robert Silvey, the Head of Audience Research, in a report he wrote titled 'The Impact of BBC2', after four years of transmission, only 13.5 million people could receive the station.

BELOW: *Play School* stars Humpty and Jemima saw their show become the first ever broadcast on BBC2.

Looking back from an age when most sitcoms fall at the first hurdle, never making it beyond the opening series, the 1960s appear as a fecund period: an abundance of golden nuggets emerged, well-polished specimens of sitcom writing at its best. Sure, there were duff shows just like any other era, but there was a noticeable crop of excellent series from the pens of fine scriptwriters, with no better example than Home Guard favourite, *Dad's Army*, which marched into the schedules in July 1968. Becoming a mainstay of the BBC schedules for the next nine years, nine series and three Christmas Specials were transmitted. The show, thanks to endless repeats, has become a cult classic, venerated by scriptwriters and the viewing public.

OPPOSITE: John Alderton and Deryck Guyler crossed swords in *Please, Sir!* in 1968.

BELOW: In the 1960s Sid James (the one on the left) was one of British television's most popular comedy stars.

From the pens of Jimmy Perry and David Croft, who later provided us with *It Ain't Half Hot, Mum*, *Hi-de-Hi!* and *You Rang, M'Lord?*, eighty episodes of *Dad's Army* spotlighted the adventures of the Walmington Home Guard, headed by the seaside town's pompous bank manager, George Mainwaring. The characters, who included Jones, Pike, Walker, Frazer, Godfrey and, of course, the languid Sergeant Wilson, were brought to life by a troupe mainly consisting of veteran character actors whose experience and abilities had been founded on years of hard work in repertory theatres up and down the country.

Each of Perry and Croft's characters was finely drawn, with never a weak link in sight, which helps to explain the show's longevity. They were brilliantly portrayed by the actors, particularly Arthur Lowe who played the portly Captain Mainwaring. He stamped his inimitable style on the character, so much so that it's difficult to imagine any actor other than Lowe being considered for the part, but others were, as Jimmy Perry explains: 'I claim credit for Arthur Lowe. I kept telling David he should be in the show but the BBC weren't convinced, particularly Michael Mills. I remember him saying, "Arthur Lowe? We don't know him at the BBC, he doesn't work for us."'

Lowe was earning many plaudits for his portrayal of Mr Swindley in Granada's *Coronation Street,* but the trouble was that Lowe's small-screen

BELOW: *Dad's Army* stormed onto TV in 1968 and has been defending its beachhead ever since.

reputation had been built around success primarily in commercial television, not at the Beeb.

When it came to casting the role of Mainwaring, actor Thorley Walters headed the wish list but when he declined, Jon Pertwee, later of *Doctor Who* fame, was the next target. Pertwee, who'd seen the original script and showed an interest, was pursued by the BBC but they failed to get their man. Much to Perry's delight, Arthur Lowe was finally invited to meet Michael Mills, David Croft (who also produced the show) and Jimmy Perry. After lengthy discussions, the part was eventually offered and *Dad's Army* was on its way.

The idea for the show was conceived by Jimmy Perry back in 1967. Then a young actor, his only experience of writing involved pantomimes and comedy sketches. While travelling by train to the East London suburb of Stratford, where he was working for Joan Littlewood's theatre company, he started nurturing ideas for a new sitcom.

'I kept telling myself that I must write for television because I could create a good part for myself – that was the main reason for writing *Dad's Army*,' he laughs.

Realizing the importance of writing from experience, he turned his attention to the Home Guard, in which he'd served at Barnes and Watford during the Second World War. He wrote a script, titled *The Fighting Tigers*, before putting it to one side for several weeks. When he later appeared in an episode of *Beggar My Neighbour*, he asked the producer, David Croft, to read his attempt at scriptwriting. Croft agreed, and before long the green light had been given to film the first series of this wartime classic.

Beggar My Neighbour, incidentally, emerged from *Comedy Playhouse*, a vehicle for testing out pilot scripts. David Croft produced two of three series transmitted between 1967 and 1968. Written by Ken Hoare and Michael Sharland, and starring Peter Jones (replaced by Desmond Walter-Ellis after series one), June Whitfield, Reg Varney and Pat Coombs, the 'Keeping-up-with-the-Joneses' sitcom focused on married sisters Rose and Lana, who happened to live next door to each other in Muswell Hill, London, and whose husbands were at either end of the pay spectrum in their respective jobs.

Examining what made the show such a success with critics and viewers, David Croft says it was 'the snobbishness of Peter Jones and his screen wife, played by June Whitfield, as they tried to succeed in the upmarket world, next door to Reg Varney and his wife, who were real workers. It was great fun.'

Reg Varney and Peter Jones were being reunited after originally working together on *The Rag Trade*. Exploring life inside the workshop of Fenner Fashion, the sitcom, written

'I kept telling myself that I must write for television because I could create a good part for myself.'

by Ronald Wolfe and Ronald Chesney, had us in stitches for two years. It was a format the writers later revisited in 1969, with *Wild, Wild Women*, evolving from another *Comedy Playhouse* episode, starring Barbara Windsor, Paul Whitsun-Jones and Pat Coombs. *The Rag Trade*, meanwhile, ran to three series on the BBC between 1961 and 1963, with Jones playing Harold Fenner, owner of the firm, and Varney as Reg, the foreman. Much of the humour stemmed from Fenner's constant confrontations with Paddy, played by Miriam Karlin, the trade union shop steward. Jones and Karlin later reprised their roles when Wolfe and Chesney wrote two further series for London Weekend Television in the late seventies.

The Rag Trade notched up a number of 'firsts' for the Beeb because it was the first series based in a dress factory and the first time Wolfe and Chesney had

ABOVE: Miriam Karlin reprised her role as Paddy, *The Rag Trade*'s shop steward, for a revival of the show in 1977.

written a series for television. An enthusiastic Dennis Main Wilson, as director, remarked in the *Radio Times* in October 1961 that he was particularly proud that 'all the factory's machines [sewing machines] work, and all the cast taking part have been trained to use them professionally.'

The original series travelled well and was shown around the world. In Australia, a ratings analysis on Sydney's ABN-2 station confirmed *The Rag Trade*, which had a working title of *The Dress Factory*, was the most watched programme on local television. In the UK, over 14 million regularly tuned in with Miriam Karlin, Esma Cannon and Sheila Hancock receiving sackloads of fan mail. Karlin, playing the troublesome shop steward who constantly called her union workers out on strike by blowing a whistle, told the *Radio Times* in March 1962 that it was difficult getting away from the attention. 'Even on holiday in Majorca, people came up to me and said: "Where's your whistle, love?"'

For the final series, number three, the show lost two of its most popular characters: Lily, played by the diminutive Esma Cannon, and

OPPOSITE: *Rag Trade* star Barbara Windsor leads Sylvia Syms, fellow *Rag Trader* Miriam Karlin, Rita Moreno and Millicent Martin in rehearsal for a stage appearance in 1964.

AROUND THE WORLD 1962

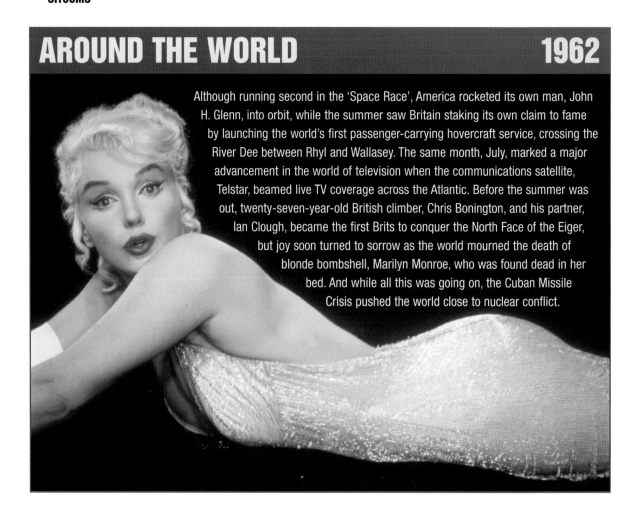

Although running second in the 'Space Race', America rocketed its own man, John H. Glenn, into orbit, while the summer saw Britain staking its own claim to fame by launching the world's first passenger-carrying hovercraft service, crossing the River Dee between Rhyl and Wallasey. The same month, July, marked a major advancement in the world of television when the communications satellite, Telstar, beamed live TV coverage across the Atlantic. Before the summer was out, twenty-seven-year-old British climber, Chris Bonington, and his partner, Ian Clough, became the first Brits to conquer the North Face of the Eiger, but joy soon turned to sorrow as the world mourned the death of blonde bombshell, Marilyn Monroe, who was found dead in her bed. And while all this was going on, the Cuban Missile Crisis pushed the world close to nuclear conflict.

Carole, brought to life by Sheila Hancock. Some new faces were introduced to the workforce, including Barbara Windsor as Judy, just before she made her *Carry On* debut in 1964's *Spying*. Director Dennis Main Wilson was pleased with the casting, as he mentioned in a memo to the Head of Light Entertainment in December 1962. Summarizing his opinions of Windsor, he said: 'Fully justified the gamble in casting her for a major part. Has the comedy personality and immediate impact, which will go a long way to fill the vacuum left by Esma Cannon.'

Two years after quitting Fenner Fashions, Sheila Hancock was back working with writers Wolfe and Chesney in her own sitcom, *The Bedsit Girl*. The writers were commissioned at £600 per script to write the series as a vehicle for Hancock. In their original proposal, Wolfe and Chesney described the show as 'a half-hour situation comedy based on the experiences of a girl from out of town, living in a cheap bedsit in a house round Bayswater way. Feeling that she was missing something in her small home town, she had come to London against the wishes of her parents, to whom she continually writes reassuring letters . . . in fact, she's having a continual struggle against loneliness, making ends meet, holding down jobs, fighting off predatory males.' The BBC show ran to two series, between 1965 and 1966, before Hancock waved goodbye to bedsit land for pastures new.

Sheila Hancock renewed her acquaintance with Peter Jones, with whom she'd worked on *The Rag Trade*, in 1969's *Mr Digby, Darling*. Written by *Beggar My Neighbour* writers Ken Hoare and Michael Sharland for Yorkshire Television, the show extended to twenty episodes, transmitted in three series between 1969 and 1970. Hancock was cast as Thelma Teesdale, an ultra-efficient secretary employed at Rid-O-Rat, a pesticide manufacturer, to take care of bungling boss Roland Digby's every need. Jones played Digby in this pleasing sitcom and the writers enjoyed working with him again.

As Sharland says: 'We could have gone on writing *Beggar My Neighbour* but got an offer to go to Yorkshire TV, which was in its infancy back then. We wanted to work with Peter again and Yorkshire offered us a lot more money than we were getting at the BBC – that influenced us, of course.'

Sharland explains the idea behind *Mr Digby, Darling*. 'It was about a man who almost had a home in the office. He had a relationship with his secretary which, although there was a total absence of sex, was like a marriage; she turned the office into a home for him, and it was much better than what he had with his actual wife.'

One of the longest-running sitcoms during the sixties was John Chapman's *Hugh and I*, which ran on the BBC between 1962 and 1968. Seventy-nine episodes were spread over seven series and starred Terry Scott as a dreaming bachelor continually concocting impossible schemes in an attempt to earn his fortune. Hugh Lloyd played a down-to-earth lodger who worked at the local factory. Both characters lived with Scott's screen mother at 33 Lobelia Avenue, Tooting, London.

After five series, Lloyd and Scott were ready to call it day but were persuaded to carry on. Changes were introduced, though: the cosy suburban setting was swapped for different backdrops, with the sixth season based around a world cruise and the final series, retitled *Hugh and I Spy*, seeing the pair returning from their holidays.

David Croft produced all but the sixth series and found it an enjoyable show to work on. 'The scripts always arrived early and Terry and Hugh were very professional so it was pretty easy. Terry always wanted things right, quite understandably, and wouldn't stand any mucking about. It was a little difficult because he was partially deaf in one ear and if people didn't speak up when giving him his cues, he got terribly cross.

'He always thought Hugh Lloyd completed things very easily and wasn't taking it seriously enough. Hugh was, of course – he was every bit as on the ball as Terry was. They got on well, though. Living close together,

Terry used to collect Hugh in his car and en route to the studio they would go through their scenes, playing their parts. They were great to work with. They knew all their lines by about Thursday and we'd then head to the local restaurant and have a great lunch.'

Working as production manager on *Hugh and I Spy* was Harold Snoad, who later directed such popular sitcoms as *Rings on Their Fingers*, *Don't Wait Up*, *Ever Decreasing Circles*, *Brush Strokes* and *Keeping Up Appearances*. He recalls a tricky sequence in the final episode which saw Terry and Hugh supposedly attending an investiture ceremony at Buckingham Palace. 'The action required them to be seen arriving at the Palace and then during the actual ceremony spotting two of the "enemy" – who had been chasing them throughout the series – disguised as footmen. As a result, we needed to see a terrified Terry and Hugh beating a very hasty retreat by running across the forecourt of the Palace, out the gates and down the Mall.

'As the show's production manager it was my job to sort out the logistics so that we could film the necessary action. I had no problem finding a large, impressive function room in a property in St James's Square for the investiture apparently taking place *inside* Buckingham Palace, but the action *outside* the Palace wasn't so easy. I spoke to the Lord Chamberlain's office who, whilst sympathetic, said they regrettably couldn't give us permission to film at the gates or in the forecourt – otherwise, they said, the next thing would be someone wanting to shoot a margarine commercial outside!

'I realized that, if we were going to finish up with the material we needed, we obviously had to be a bit devious. I came up with an idea and looked at some newsreel footage of cars arriving for a recent investiture. We then hired the same model of car and temporarily changed the number plate on our car to match the one on film, the idea being that having taken a long shot of our car coming up the Mall, we'd have a camera in the front seat looking towards Terry and Hugh sitting in the back. Through the window behind them we could see that the car was coming from the Mall and passing the Victoria Memorial on its way to the Palace gates. At the appropriate point we could cut to the newsreel shot and what would apparently be the same car sweeping through the gates into the Palace forecourt.

'On the day, having taken the long shot of our car in the Mall, it was parked up by St James's Palace with the cameraman now in the front looking back at Terry and Hugh. I was outside the left-hand side of the two Palace gates and in contact – via a walkie-talkie – with the car. I set the car off and then walked over and had a word with a policeman on duty, explaining that our car wouldn't actually enter the forecourt but would drive up fairly fast prior to stopping in the entrance (if it slowed down too much it wouldn't have cut properly to the speed of the car on the newsreel footage).

LEFT: Terry Scott and
Hugh Lloyd with
Margaret Nolan in *Hugh
and I*, 1966.

'The policeman looked a bit worried and said he would have to go away and check this out – presumably not having taken on board that I'd said the car would be arriving any minute. He walked off to another area and wasn't even present when our vehicle came up and stopped abruptly at the gate! I hurried Terry and Hugh from the car, which then reversed and pulled up on the other side of the road where the cameraman hastily got his gear out.

'In the meantime I told Terry and Hugh (who, of course, were in full morning suits) to join the crowds looking through the railings and discreetly make their way along to the right-hand gate.

'I then got my assistant, who was Scottish, to engage the constable standing on the right-hand side of that gate in conversation by asking him, in the broadest Scottish accent, directions to Clarence House. This involved the constable turning away to look down the Mall, at which point I ushered Terry and Hugh through the gate and they started walking across the forecourt. They were almost at the inner gate when the

DO YOU REMEMBER THE TEST CARD GIRL?

Most people who watched TV in the sixties will remember the little girl playing noughts and crosses on the test card, but may never have known her name. She was Carole Hersee and first appeared in July 1967 on BBC2, although the picture had been taken the previous December. She holds the honour of being the most seen person on TV.

With the arrival of colour transmission, the Beeb required a new test card. Deciding upon a human element this time, a committee, chaired by the late engineer George Hersee, opted for George's eight-year-old daughter. 'I didn't mind doing it but was teased a lot at school, which upset me,' says Carole Hersee, now in her forties, who was the recipient of an award by the Royal Television Society for helping to sell so many TVs. The test card, which was seen as far afield as Hong Kong, was used to help tune the set, but nobody expected that Test Card F, to use its technical classification, would last so long.

Upon completing her education, Carole pursued a career making theatrical costumes, which she still does today. Her creations have blessed numerous films and West End productions, such as *The Phantom of the Opera*.

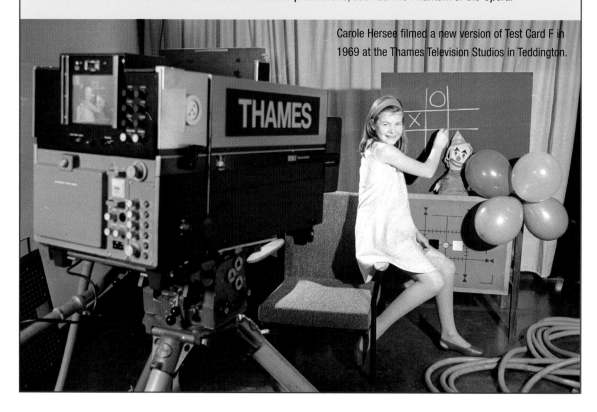

Carole Hersee filmed a new version of Test Card F in 1969 at the Thames Television Studios in Teddington.

policeman noticed and shouted for them to come back. As planned, they turned and ran from the Palace across the forecourt, out the gate past the policeman, through the traffic and down the Mall, the action being captured as I had planned by our cameraman. We immediately rendezvoused on the Albert Memorial – everybody grabbing various bits of equipment – as I used my walkie-talkie to summon the two taxis I had waiting on Constitution Hill. We all piled in and were away in less than two minutes. I rather expected that there would be some immediate comeback, but when the Lord Chamberlain's office finally rang the next day, they said, "Well done, but don't do it again!" The sequence cut together very well and we finished up with just what we needed.'

Although *Hugh and I* was one of the first series David Croft produced after joining the Beeb from Tyne Tees Television, he cut his BBC teeth on 1961's seven-part series *The Eggheads*, starring Bryan Blackburn, Peter Reeves, Robert Jackson and Vivien Grant as students. In his autobiography, *You Have Been Watching . . .*, Croft recalls the day he was asked to see Frank Muir and Denis Norden, who were working as comedy advisers in the Beeb's light-entertainment division. 'They told me they had been nursing a new project that they were thrilled about, based on the life and background of university students. They had contacted a few writers who had attempted scripts, and the whole project was to go on air in four weeks' time.' The fact Croft hadn't attended university didn't concern Muir and Norden and they were confident he'd do a good job. He adds: 'Being new to the BBC, as I left their office I failed to hear the loud sigh of relief at having unloaded this particular turkey.' The series, which began poorly in terms of audience reaction, recovered some pride but after seven episodes was dropped.

As *The Eggheads* retreated into their shells, ABC television was commissioning a second series of *Our House*, which ran between 1960 and 1962. Fresh from big-screen success with the first three *Carry On* scripts (*Sergeant*, *Nurse* and *Teacher*), writer Norman Hudis was approached by agent Harry Foster and his client, award-winning television director Ernest Maxin, to write a television series using some of the *Carry On* films' actors. Within two hours, Hudis and Maxin developed a premise for the series.

'It was about a group of disparate people unable individually to afford a house, pooling their resources to buy a property,' Hudis explains. 'We wrote specifically for *Carry On* alumni Hattie Jacques, Joan Sims, Charles Hawtrey and Norman Rossington. All agreed to sign on, without seeing a single script, when told I was to be the writer. This felt good and I'm not going to be falsely modest about it. One gets kicked in the ass so often in this business that there's no swelling of the head when one is patted on it!'

Our House was swiftly sold to ABC, with a thirteen-script commitment and an hour time slot, unusual in the world of situation comedy. 'We were originally supposed to air at about 6.00 p.m.,' says Hudis, 'but there was some inter-network dispute and we were relegated to 3.25 p.m. on

'All agreed to sign on, without seeing a single script, when told I was to be the writer. One gets kicked in the ass so often in this business that there's no swelling of the head when one is patted on it!'

'What sort of characters am I playing this week?'

Sundays, in which slot we achieved our one appearance in the ratings – number 20 out of 20, when we were up against Portuguese football: formidable opposition indeed.'

As in his work on the *Carry Ons*, Hudis wasn't afraid to use a touch of pathos rather than going all-out for laughs – *Carry On Sergeant* and *Carry On Teacher*, in particular, contain moments of high emotion as well as their fair share of laughs. He says: 'I followed my instincts, and was backed by Ernest Maxin, in doing without overt comedy for a few moments in some episodes, where the human values accented sentiment and emotion rather than guffaws.

'My feeling was that such conventional demands as "You've got to have four laughs a page" killed my invention stone-dead. Yes, this was a comedy series, but when a moment wasn't legitimately funny, forget the rules. A genuine lump in the throat is often more effective than an enforced split side.'

Sadly, ABC television eventually erased all but two of the first season's tapes which, despite the height of the *Carry On* success in the United States, destroyed any possibility of an American sale that would have garnered royalties for all.

Despite inter-network feuding culminating in *Our House* being relegated to the unflattering Sunday afternoon slot, ABC were soon commissioning another season, this time consisting of twenty-six hour-long episodes, a tall order for any writer or director. Ernest Maxin says: 'Editing hadn't really come in to any great effect, so I had to shoot each show as live, with each having about 250 camera shots of different angles. You'd be one side of the studio shooting a sequence while the crew were changing the set on the other side, hoping they'd finish before you got to it. It was a great experience and Norman wrote some terrific scripts.'

When the second series was commissioned, Norman Hudis was temporarily released from his contract with *Carry On* film producer Peter Rogers, in order to complete the set of scripts.

'I was determined to have all twenty-six scripts in good shape before rehearsals began,' he says. 'Consulting Ernest about themes, I achieved this aim – unprecedented at the time – including a full musical. Some cast changes occurred and I tried to cater for them. But things weren't the same. Harry Korris and Hylda Baker [who joined the cast] were beyond my style and interest. They were, especially Baker, essentially, magnificent music-hall artists and much as I enjoyed good raucous vaudeville where, indeed, "four laughs a page and more if possible and it doesn't matter how you get 'em" was the time-honoured rule, it wasn't within my scope as a writer. It showed, though, stubbornly, I denied it at the time. Of the twenty-six scripts I wrote, five were produced, twenty-one heartily disliked and rejected.

'Two other writers, Brad Ashton and Bob Block, were brought in and, in true pressured TV style, their new scripts were virtually written in the rehearsal room during the week culminating in their airing. Ernest Maxin, my friend to this day, rose to the crisis magnificently. It was just the sort of challenge to which he responded. What was our character-driven *Our House* became a personality romp for Charles Hawtrey and Hylda Baker.'

Maxin, who acknowledges the pressures both Hudis and he were under on *Our House*, explains: 'These were one-hour shows. The first thirteen were okay but it gets very hard after that. Norman and I having to think up new ideas; it was very draining for both of us. Two other writers were brought in but I feel it didn't have the same individuality of the first series because it was so different. The second series lacked the charm of the first. Norman and I created the show together, but when you bring in other people, they don't have the same feeling for it.'

Hawtrey and Baker were so successful that they later got their own series, *Best of Friends*. It ran for thirteen episodes in 1963, telling the story of Charles, an insurance office clerk, and Hylda, who ran a café next door. Written by Brad Ashton and Bob Block, it was produced by Ernest Maxin.

Although not strictly situation comedy, *The Dick Emery Show*, which began its eighteen-year run on BBC in 1963, saw David Croft and Harold Snoad credited among the many producers allocated to the sketch show during its long life. Snoad, however, stayed the longest – eight years. He found working with Emery both 'fascinating' and 'a challenge'. Harold says: 'We turned out some memorable shows together, attaining very high viewing figures – sometimes around 15 million and, in one case, 21 million!

'In my early days working with Dick, I remember that we would send him the script for the next show but when he arrived in the rehearsal room he still hadn't opened the envelope! He would sit down alongside me for the read-through and say: "What sort of characters am I playing this week?" I realized pretty quickly that one of the reasons for his extremely laid-back attitude was that the sketches were not only much too

BELOW: Dick Emery enjoyed eighteen years at the BBC with his comedy show.

ABOVE: Former coal miner Harry Worth first had his own national TV series in 1960.

long but had far too many people in them. This latter point meant that the other parts were, inevitably, fairly small and, therefore, being cast with people who posed no "threat" whatsoever to Dick.

'I decided to change this and asked a number of well-known writers to come up with shorter sketches with only two or three characters. I will never forget the day Dick walked into the rehearsal room and stopped dead in his tracks when he spotted Richard Todd, who was a pretty big name in the film world. Dick grabbed hold of me and whispered: "What's he doing here?" When I told him that Richard was in a two-handed sketch with him he literally tore open the envelope. The new policy worked well and I subsequently brought in Roy Kinnear and Pat Coombs on a fairly regular basis plus occasional appearances from other well-known faces.'

Another comedy actor who, like Emery, moved through a series of programme formats was Harry Worth, who began his working life as a coal miner at the age of fourteen. He turned to the world of entertainment after serving in the Second World War, starring in his first national television series, *The Trouble with Harry*, in 1960. The same year, the first of seven series of *Here's Harry*, which would run until 1965, was screened. Creating most of the scripts were writing partners Vince Powell and Harry Driver, who between them would go on to write a host of hit sitcoms. Powell remembers the day producer John Ammonds rang offering them the chance of writing the series. 'Johnnie explained, "The BBC have said I can do a half-hour pilot for a situation comedy, would you like to write it?" I said "yes", but when I asked who it was for, he said, "It's for a ventriloquist!" Harry Worth worked as a ventriloquist then, but I thought: "How the bloody hell do you write for a ventriloquist?"'

Nevertheless, writers Powell and Driver wrote a successful pilot and were commissioned for five more episodes. When asked to describe the series, Powell refers to the pilot episode. 'It all hinged on that first show where he left his umbrella on a bus and went to the lost property office. He told the chap in the office that he'd left it on the number twenty-nine bus, but when asked to describe it, replied: "It was a red double-decker with four wheels." And that was Harry Worth, always getting the wrong end of the stick.'

One of the most memorable aspects of the sitcom was the opening title sequence, showing Worth using his reflection in a shop window to create an optical illusion with his limbs. It was Vince Powell who dreamt up the idea.

'I used to do it as a kid,' he smiles. 'I'd written it in the script and the producer, John Ammonds, and I went to see Harry at Blackpool, where he was performing, to discuss the show. As you can imagine, it was difficult explaining what I wanted Harry to do, so I took him outside and showed him in a window on Blackpool's promenade. Harry fell about laughing, and John said: "We must start every show with that!" As it was my idea, I got an extra seven guineas every time Harry did it.'

While *Here's Harry* was written for the BBC, Powell and Driver spent most of their sitcom careers working for various ITV stations. Prolific in the late sixties, their output included *George and the Dragon* and *Two in Clover*, as well as the Arthur Lowe vehicle, *Pardon the Expression*.

Arthur Lowe, alias Captain Mainwaring in *Dad's Army*, was playing fussy draper Leonard Swindley, a leading character in *Coronation Street*, when the writing duo decided they'd like to take the character out of the *Street* setting and base a sitcom around him. Set in a northern department

BELOW: Sid James and Peggy Mount in *George and the Dragon.*

store, where Swindley was assistant manager, thirty-six episodes of *Pardon the Expression* were transmitted by Granada in two series between 1965 and 1966. The series eventually 'ran out of steam', but Powell enjoyed writing for Arthur Lowe. 'He was an excellent actor and used to laugh at the jokes more than the audience.'

It was over lunch at Rules, London's oldest restaurant, that Powell and Driver were asked to write a show for Sid James and Peggy Mount. Producer Alan Tarrant, who was working for ATV, explained that they had James and Mount under contract and were searching for a suitable vehicle. The writers came up with *George and the Dragon*, starring James, Mount, John Le Mesurier and Keith Marsh. Playing his trademark lecherous character, Sid James was George Russell, chauffeur to Colonel Maynard. The good Colonel had seen a succession of chambermaids and cooks scared off by Russell's sexual advances, until the appropriately named Gabrielle Dragon joined the household.

George and the Dragon ran to four series from 1966 to 1968, by which time Powell and Driver were already busy writing *Never Mind the Quality, Feel the Width* for Thames Television, a sitcom about Irish and Jewish tailors who combine forces. While they were waiting to hear whether a new series of *George and the Dragon* would be commissioned, Philip Jones, Head of Entertainment at Thames, offered Powell and Driver exclusive contracts to write thirteen scripts a year, and to act as comedy advisers on ideas submitted to his department. They accepted like a shot. 'The next day, the phone rang and it was Sid James,' recalls Powell. 'He said: "I've got great news. I've just heard from my agent that Lew Grade wants to do another thirteen *George and the Dragon*s." When we told him we couldn't do them because we'd just signed the exclusive contract, he replied, "Right, I'll come to Thames." It was a great compliment to us as writers.'

Their next show for Sid James was *Two in Clover*, with James cast as Sid Turner and Victor Spinetti as Vic Evans, two clerks so fed up working for an insurance company that they did a Tom Good (although it was six years before *The Good Life* was born) and decided to live off the land on a smallholding in the village of Fletchley. Two series were made (1969-70) before the show was dropped. 'The trouble was, in the first series we tried to recreate a farm in the studio,' says Vince Powell. 'We had cows in pens but they kept crapping and piddling all over the floor, but it got a lot of laughs. We then decided to do it mostly on film, but it became too expensive.' Still attempting to find the right show for Sid James, they struck gold with their next attempt, *Bless This House*, which began in 1971.

Before the decade was out, Powell and Driver had written a pilot and three episodes of *Nearest and Dearest* for Granada, depicting life inside a pickle factory; unfortunately, their exclusive contract with Thames prevented them continuing with the series and other writers were brought in. One of the partnership's less successful shows was *Best of Enemies*, shown in 1968 and 1969, which focused on opposing politicians having to share an office at Westminster. The programme wasn't liked by Thames's Philip Jones and was quickly put out of its misery after just five episodes.

Sid James was one of the business's best-loved comedy actors, adored by the public and industry insiders alike. During the sixties his craggy features were rarely off the screen, as he appeared in television shows and numerous films. Written specially for him by Ray Galton and Alan Simpson, *Citizen James* was the writers' way of acknowledging James's contribution to *Hancock's Half Hour*, from which he'd been unceremoniously dumped due to Tony Hancock's desire to go it alone. Adopting the same persona he mastered in *Hancock's Half Hour*, Sidney Balmoral James remained a wide boy throughout the three series (1960 to 1962), but this time lived in Soho rather than East Cheam. Galton and Simpson wrote much of the first series in an office at Elstree Studios while making the Hancock film, *The Rebel*, before leaving the show in the capable hands of Sid Green and Dick Hills and moving on to *Steptoe and Son*.

The country's most famous rag-and-bone men, Albert and Harold Steptoe, started life as part of a *Comedy Playhouse* series written by Galton and Simpson, who'd been friends since recovering from

'He was an excellent actor and used to laugh at the jokes more than the audience.'

BELOW: The country's most popular junk merchants, *Steptoe and Son*, first appeared in 1962.

tuberculosis at the same Surrey sanatorium. Soon after finishing *Hancock*, they met with the BBC's Tom Sloan to discuss their future, as Alan Simpson explains. 'He asked what we wanted to do next so we told him – a series with Frankie Howerd. He replied, "No, you don't want to do that, he's finished. We did a series with him and had terrible figures. I don't think we want that." He then told us about his title, *Comedy Playhouse*, and said we could fill the ten weeks by writing anything we wanted. "You can be in it, direct it, do whatever you like." It was a lovely opportunity – no writer had been given carte blanche like that before. It was too good an offer to refuse.'

Worryingly, though, by the time they reached number four in the series, their ideas had dried up. Simpson recalls: 'We couldn't think of anything. We spent three or four days just hoping a suitable idea would turn up. The trouble is, when people say you can do what you like, you have nothing to hang it on – no personality or subject. In those days, if we couldn't think of anything, we'd amuse ourselves by making outrageous suggestions which couldn't possibly work, like having two rat catchers in Buckingham Palace. Ray said one morning, "Two rag-and-bone men with a horse and cart going down Piccadilly." We laughed because it was another outrageous suggestion.

'Three hours later, we revisited the idea and started thinking that perhaps it could work. We began writing and ended up with ten pages about these two men arguing in their yard.'

From that moment, *Steptoe and Son* evolved, and it was Galton and Simpson who suggested Harry H. Corbett and Wilfrid Brambell to play the scruffy, filthy rag-and-bone men. When Brambell arrived for the first read-through, the writers were in for a shock. 'We couldn't believe it when this immaculately dressed man walked in with this terribly posh voice. But we'd seen him playing old cockney men, so knew he could do it. He wore false teeth so had a set blackened and stained. When we finished recording, he'd go into his dressing room and within half an hour emerge like a butterfly from a chrysalis – totally transformed wearing beautiful clothes, highly polished shoes, an overcoat draped over his shoulders, a homburg hat and carrying a cane with a silver top. Harry, meanwhile, seemed to dress better in the show than off it!' *Steptoe and Son*, originating from Galton and Simpson's *Comedy Playhouse* instalment *The Offer*, ran to eight series between 1962 and 1974 before Galton and Simpson called time. It's now regarded as a true classic of the genre.

One of the grittiest sitcoms to hit our screens during the sixties was *The Likely Lads*. Focusing on the lives of two working-class lads from the north-east, Bob Ferris and Terry Collier (played by Rodney Bewes and James Bolam), twenty-one episodes were made between 1965 and 1966. A decade later, the Lads reunited – perhaps even more successfully – for a sequel, *Whatever Happened to the Likely Lads?*

The series began life as a short film made by Dick Clement, who wrote the series with Ian La Frenais, as part of a directors' training course he attended at the BBC. Clement worked as a studio manager at the Beeb but had aspirations for directing. Little did he know that when he attended the course, his roll of celluloid costing just £100 would lead to a new career as a scriptwriter. Bill Cotton, who was in charge of the directors' course, spotted its potential and advised Michael Peacock, BBC2's first Chief of Programmes, to watch it. Peacock recalls: 'He [Cotton] was very excited and wanted me to see a film in his office. He had a 16mm projector and was projecting it onto the wall.' Peacock was suitably impressed. 'Here was a show that was clearly chock-a-block with promise. I immediately told Bill we should go for a series, and we did.'

Clement and La Frenais never regarded their plans of spotlighting two lads-about-town as original, but they were treading into uncharted areas in some respects. 'Nobody had portrayed the North or the working classes in situation comedy,' says Clement. 'We'd been influenced by all those British black-and-white films of the period: *Saturday Night and Sunday*

BELOW: Bewes and Bolam were reunited in the seventies for *Whatever Happened to the Likely Lads?*

Morning, *Billy Liar* and *A Kind of Loving*, all bringing a breath of fresh air to the British cinema. Ian and I wanted to do the same for television.'

The first of three series kicked off in December 1964. Dick Clement recalls: '*The Likely Lads* was the first professional work that Ian and I did together. That alone gave it a special adrenalin rush, together with a sense of disbelief. On top of that, when I was asked to direct the shows, too, I had suddenly stumbled into the perfect situation that people strive for years to attain. I should have been terrified, but I was protected by ignorance.

'I was further cushioned by two factors. First by Syd Lotterby, who was

THE DOORS OPEN AT THE NEW BBC HQ

The BBC kicked off the sixties with the grand opening of their spanking new offices at Television Centre in London's Shepherd's Bush. Six years in the making, the building was described in the *Radio Times* on 24 June 1960 as 'a giant bowl of bricks and glass and concrete and mosaic' – not the most complimentary description in the world. One of the benefits for the Beeb was that it allowed immediate access from the scenery block, enabling scenery to be shifted from the BBC's workshop direct to the studio within minutes. The *Radio Times'* reporter compared a tour of the Centre to being taken around a 'large ocean liner'. The grand opening was celebrated in a Wednesday evening show, *First Night*. For the first time in its history the BBC was able to work from a purpose-built home instead of converted film studios at Lime Grove and Hammersmith, an old variety theatre renamed the Television Theatre and, of course, Alexandra Palace.

assigned as my production assistant. He was far more experienced than I was and many people in that situation would have "come the old soldier", sat back and watched me flounder. On the contrary, he shielded me and helped me with extraordinary generosity. The second factor, in a perverse way, was neglect. The show was clearly a schedule filler. Nobody expected it to achieve anything and consequently nobody bothered us – quite literally. None of the top brass attended any of the rehearsals or recordings. At the time, we felt faintly hurt. In hindsight, it was infinitely preferable to the alternative – endless notes from the legions of Network Executives.

'On the night of the first recording, Ian was standing behind me in the "gallery" as I stared glassy-eyed at the bank of screens. When we got our first laugh I turned round to share the moment with him – and missed about four shots. I was saved again by professionalism. Clive Doig, the vision mixer, kept cutting without me, as per script. I was a useless ornament for the rest of the show, my brain trying to catch up, but still dazzled by every reaction from the studio audience below.'

Although first transmitted on BBC2, it was the sitcom's repeat on BBC1 three months later that exposed it to a much wider audience. In the process it made names of the show's leading actors, Rodney Bewes and James Bolam.

'The reaction from the public was fantastic,' says Bewes. 'My family were really pleased, too, and lots of my relatives would come along to recordings. Being recognized and receiving fan mail was amazing. But the best reaction was when people said: "The Lads are just like we used to be." Fellas identified so much with Bob and Terry, just one reason it became a success.'

We waved goodbye to the Geordie lads on 23 July 1966 – or so everyone thought, including Clement and La Frenais, who hadn't an inkling that they'd be revisiting their small-screen creations as the lads approached middle age in the seventies' sequel, *Whatever Happened to...?* Back in 1966, both writers were ready for pastures new. 'We were getting offers in other directions,' says Clement. 'We thought three series was enough, so did the actors.'

La Frenais adds: 'I could have probably done another series, but the boys were talking about film careers, as if doing seven or eight episodes of *The Likely Lads* affected things. It was a time when television was building an audience, as well as TV stars, and with that came the worry for actors that if they did too much television, they'd never be offered anything else.'

Rodney Bewes's next long run on the small screen, three years after *The Likely Lads* finished, was in a series he wrote and produced with Derrick Goodwin. On 15 September 1969, the first of four series of *Dear Mother . . . Love Albert* was transmitted by Thames Television with Bewes playing Albert Courtnay. The premise of the series came from Bewes's real-life letters home to his mother, reflecting on his daily life. Bewes was happy with the show's success. 'It did well, averaging number seven in the ratings.' Yet it was while he was enduring the rigours of flu that Bewes came up with the idea for the sitcom. Having been bed-bound for over a week, he reached for pen and paper and started scribbling a note to his mother. 'I've always been a tremendous letter writer, and I wrote saying: "I'm having such a great time here in London: I went out with Ian [La Frenais] last night; he collected me in his Rolls-Royce, and he went down the King's Road to an Italian restaurant and Princess Margaret was there." You never write home with bad news, else your mother would be on the next train. Suddenly it gave me an idea for a series, where each episode began with a weekly letter home to mum, saying how well I was doing . . . and showing the opposite!'

After recuperating, Bewes had lunch with Philip Jones, Head of Light Entertainment at Thames Television, explaining his concept. Enamoured of the idea, Jones commissioned a series and Bewes played the lead. When Thames were unable to make the second season, Yorkshire Television picked up the show and it ran for three more series until Bewes was faced with a dilemma. Clement and La Frenais had already floated the idea of bringing Bob and Terry – alias *The Likely Lads* – back to the small screen, but if Bewes agreed to return, it signalled the end for *Dear Mother* . . . 'I was writing, producing and doing very well; it was also incredibly lucrative. But I knew in my heart of hearts I longed to do *Whatever Happened to the Likely Lads?*' His decision was made.

One of today's kings of sitcom, affable Richard Briers, who's best known for playing Tom Good in *The Good Life* and Martin Bryce in *Ever Decreasing Circles*, launched his career in situation comedy during the sixties. In 1962, Henry Cecil's book, *Brothers in Law*, which had already been adapted for the big screen by the Boulting Brothers, was made into a sitcom. With scripts by, among others, Frank Muir

BELOW: Richard Briers, pictured here with another rising comedy star of the sixties, Ronnie Barker.

and Denis Norden, Briers was cast as the young, rather green barrister, Roger Thursby, with Richard Waring playing his colleague and friend, Henry Blagrove.

Briers had previously worked with Muir and Norden in the comedy series, *Faces of Jim*, which had been written for Jimmy Edwards. Three seasons of individual comedies were screened between 1961 and 1963 with Briers appearing in three instalments. Now, with *Brothers in Law*, Briers was heading the cast, which, at times, was rather frightening for the twenty-eight-year-old.

'We made thirteen episodes and could have done more but I found the pressure too great. Then, they didn't do six or seven shows and take a break before the next series, they did them all on the trot!' he says. 'It was hell and I found the stress pretty bad. That's why we didn't do any more.'

Although his screen life as a barrister was short-lived, Briers became friends with Richard Waring and when the writer and actor began developing an idea for a new sitcom, he asked Briers to play the lead. 'It was about a young couple who got married and experienced all the problems a young couple face. They then have a baby and the man can't cope and so on. It was a great success, focusing on a charming couple and their struggles through early married life.'

So, a year after *Brothers in Law*, Richard Briers was playing George Starling, a junior clerk in the City, in *Marriage Lines*. Playing his wife, Kate, was Prunella Scales. With each of the forty-five episodes concentrating on everyday issues, audiences soon warmed to the newly-weds, empathizing, perhaps, with the Starlings as they tried to get ahead in life. Briers enjoyed the series. 'Richard Waring got to know me well and was able to write for my nervous style.'

To help promote the programme's launch in August 1963, which saw the newly-weds returning to their Earl's Court flat at three in the morning from their Paris honeymoon, Waring wrote in the *Radio Times*: 'Though it is intended as light comedy and performed before a studio audience, I have tried to give the characters depth, to make them human beings, by including straight dramatic dialogue and situations when the story demands it. After all, in real life, there are not many laughs in a "flaming row", are there?'

The opening episode, 'The Threshold', met with a warm reception according to the BBC's internal Audience Research Report, compiled after the show. The author of the report, which was based on questionnaires completed by a sample of the audience, stated: 'Richard Briers excelled at this kind of role, it was often said, and was here in his element as the harassed young husband – Prunella Scales did well, too . . . and both appeared well cast.' The sample audience welcomed a programme in

> 'It was hell and I found the stress pretty bad. That's why we didn't do any more.'

ABOVE: Prunella Scales endured a troublesome on-screen marriage long before she ever met Basil Fawlty.

which the situations were 'only slightly larger than life'. One woman commented: 'I wanted to make a cup of tea but every time I went out of the room the laughter from my husband and daughter brought me back again. In the end I turned off the kettle until the end of the show.'

While Richard Briers and Prunella Scales were establishing their TV careers in the sixties, so too were writers John Esmonde and Bob Larbey. The two would later write for Briers in *The Good Life* and *Ever Decreasing Circles*, but began achieving success on the small screen when Esmonde, a former technical journalist, and Larbey, who hated his clerical job at a printing block manufacturer, decided to have a stab at becoming professional scriptwriters over a plate of egg and chips at a Wimpy restaurant in London. Their first wages from the medium of television came when they supplied sketches for *The Dick Emery Show*, while their entrance into the genre of situation comedy was achieved in 1966 with *Room at the Bottom*. Initially a pilot was shown under the *Comedy Playhouse* umbrella, but after showing sufficient promise, a seven-part series was put in motion. With Kenneth Connor as Gus Fogg and Deryck Guyler as Mr Powell heading the cast, the programme was based around the lives of maintenance men working at a manufacturing company. They were exciting times for the writers. 'It was like the best thing that had ever happened in the entire world,' enthuses Larbey. Of watching the pilot episode, he recalls: 'It was very nail-biting. I think I was probably too nervous to laugh.'

So how did they come up with the idea for the sitcom? Bizarrely, it was staring at anonymous office blocks that sparked off an idea.

'We used to keep passing all these big buildings along Millbank, on the edge of the Thames,' explains Larbey, 'and asked ourselves the question: "Who really runs places like that?" We decided it was the maintenance men in a room at the bottom who controlled the whole thing – and that's what the sitcom was about. The maintenance men in our show were always on the fiddle, and were drawing wages for somebody who'd been dead fifteen years. When a new broom arrives and becomes suspicious, he asks the maintenance men to produce the man, and that's when the fun begins.'

Life was short for *Room at the Bottom*. It was brought to a halt after just the first season, but provided valuable experience for Esmonde and Larbey. 'It worked well, and was quite a good little story, but I don't think it was written well enough – we still had a lot to learn,' admits Larbey.

On the strength of their breakthrough in television, the writers, who'd been working in Esmonde's boxroom until that point, found an office in Dorking, and began planning their next venture. After seeing a pilot programme, *Just Good Friends*, which was transmitted as part of ABC's *Comedy Tonight* feature in 1967, fail to inspire a full-blown series, they struck gold when they headed back to the classroom in 1968 with *Please, Sir!* Watched by millions for three years, the sitcom followed the adventures of Mr Hedges, a newly-qualified teacher played by fresh-faced young actor John Alderton. He taught the infamously unruly rabble that was Class 5C at Fenn Street Secondary Modern, a tough place to cut your

AROUND THE WORLD 1963

As the British public prepared to see its rail network stripped of over 2,000 stations and the closure of many branch lines courtesy of Dr Beeching's highly controversial reports on the state of the railways, Russia was first off the blocks again when, in June, they sent the first woman into space. Summer headlines, meanwhile, were dominated by the Profumo sex scandal, which almost brought down the government, and the Great Train Robbery, where over £1 million was stolen from a train stopped at Cheddington, Buckinghamshire. This was also the tragic year when John F. Kennedy, the American President, was shot dead in Dallas. On a lighter note, the world gained a new island when Surtsey was born off the Icelandic coast following a submarine volcanic eruption.

teaching teeth. The sitcom led to a feature film and a successful spin-off, *The Fenn Street Gang*, tracing the lives of the kids after leaving school.

Between 1968 and 1972, fifty-seven episodes of *Please, Sir!* were transmitted by London Weekend Television, with Larbey and Esmonde penning all but twelve of the scripts. The idea was conceived after Frank Muir, then Head of Entertainment at London Weekend Television, consulted all the writers he'd worked with, asking for new ideas. Their first suggestion, however, was quickly given the thumbs down, as Larbey explains: 'We had this wonderful idea about a faded concert pianist who was doing end-of-the-pier work. He was living in boarding houses but refused to change his lifestyle. He was lavish with tips and sent flowers to all the girls at the end of the show. When we asked what Frank thought, he replied: "I hate that. Have you got any other ideas?" So we told him about a half-idea we'd come up with, about a young teacher at a secondary modern school, and he was interested in that straight away.'

Soon after the writers delivered a pilot script, Muir commissioned a series and secured John Alderton for the lead role. The sitcom was based in

BELOW: John Alderton with Penny Spencer in *Please, Sir!*

a rough area, where a young, callow teacher had to teach a class who knew more about the world than he did. Neither writer can recall what sparked the idea, but Larbey says: 'Being a bit young at heart, or childish, we still had a fair recall of school, the ambience and all the sounds in the corridors. The tension occurs when you stick this young idealist teacher in the position of having to teach kids who are much more worldly-wise than himself.'

Please, Sir! quickly struck a chord with viewers, surprising the writers in the process. John Esmonde says: 'We've always considered our shows to be slow-burners, but that one clicked almost immediately.' Such success engendered a sense of confidence in their abilities as professional writers. 'We were being asked to do more and more, and it was then that we started thinking: "We've actually made it. We really don't have to go back to work!"'

> 'We were being asked to do more and more, and it was then that we started thinking: "We've actually made it. We really don't have to go back to work!"'

Before we waved goodbye to the sixties, a hospital sitcom, based on a series of bestselling novels, squeezed into the schedules during July 1969. Richard Gordon, himself a doctor, wrote a number of books, beginning with *Doctor in the House*, exploiting some of his own experiences in the medical profession. Although already adapted into money-spinning films and a one-off play starring Brian Rix, which the BBC screened in 1960, nothing was to eclipse London Weekend Television's *Doctor in the House* series. Starring Barry Evans, Robin Nedwell, Geoffrey Davies and George Layton as young doctors working at the teaching hospital, St Swithin's, the storylines were only loosely connected to Gordon's popular novels; with scripts written by the likes of Graeme Garden, Bill Oddie, Graham Chapman and Barry Cryer, two series of *Doctor in the House* were screened before a succession of follow-up series, including *Doctor at Large*, *Doctor in Charge*, *Doctor at Sea* and *Doctor on the Go*, continued the momentum.

Writer and actor George Layton, who played Dr Collier, was tipped off about the new series by Christopher Timothy, alias James Herriot in *All Creatures Great and Small*. He was lucky enough to secure an audition, being the last person the director saw. 'The part I was reading for had already been cast,' explains Layton. 'Luckily, for me, they changed their minds and offered me the part of Dr Collier, although initially he was going to be called Dr Garston.' Layton – who went on to write many of the episodes with writing partner Jonathan Lynn, who'd also appear in the second series of *Doctor in the House* – regards the series as a big turning point in his career. 'I'd been around for a while, about seven years, and always thought my great strength was comedy, so it was a great break to get the part.'

When he began writing episodes, he used the pseudonym Oliver Fry, but his disguise didn't last long.

'People twigged on quite quickly, perhaps because I began interfering too much,' he admits. 'I probably became a nuisance as far as the others were concerned because if I'd written something I was very particular about how I wanted it played. Eventually I wrote myself out because I was offered *It Ain't Half Hot, Mum* and thought I'd done enough, although I continued writing for a while.'

Layton loved playing his character. 'It was a terrific part. The amorality of Dr Collier: he was totally immoral but with a certain charm – I suppose the nearest to Donald Sinden's character in the film. It was good fun and ideal family entertainment.'

What other sitcoms were trying their utmost to entertain viewers during the sixties? One title that may have slipped from your memory bank is *The Airbase*, which failed to take off in 1965. Just six episodes from the pen of American John Briley were shown by the Beeb. The show was based on the scriptwriter's own experiences of being stationed in the UK. Squadron Leader Heatherton, played by the late David Kelsey, was the top man at RAF Whittlethorpe (RAF bases North Weald and Wethersfield were used for location shooting) but most of his time was spent sorting out problems between the US servicemen, based at the station, and the locals.

As Briley detailed in his original programme format: 'Airbase will be a comic record of the fundamental problems growing out of the existence of an American airbase in a small British community. These stories will trace the adjustment of a young RAF officer to a post where he must not only live with Americans, but justify the British ways to them and, perhaps more difficult, them to the British.'

A sitcom about garden gnomes – does that fill you with uncontrollable excitement? No? Clearly the executives at the BBC thought much the same because The Gnomes of Dulwich lasted for only six episodes in 1969. Written by Jimmy Perry, co-writer of Dad's Army, It Ain't Half Hot, Mum, Hi-De-Hi! and You Rang, M'Lord?, the story revolved around a group of gnomes in the garden of 25 Telegraph Road and the clashes between the traditional British gnomes and some plastic European models which arrived in the area. Terry Scott and Hugh Lloyd were recruited to play the principal roles, for fees of £700 and £625 respectively.

When the show was launched, Perry explained: 'Garden gnomes seem to fascinate everyone. They're either amusing or repulsive, according to taste. I originally wrote a short sketch about two little stone gnomes. Had Morecambe and Wise in mind at the time. But my wife told me the idea was good enough to make a whole show.'

When Lance Percival's Lance at Large arrived in August 1964, the Radio Times hailed it as a 'new form of television comedy'. In the 6 August edition, the journalist wrote: 'The familiar moulds in which most television comedy has been cast are beginning to crumble.' Of the new style of programmes, he stated: 'Flexible, unpredictable, they have little in common except their refusal to fit any pattern at all.'

Lance Percival added: 'One of the main purposes of the series is to go outside, to see what can be done in the open as opposed to the more usual situation-comedy situation . . . The character I play, Alan Day, is just an ordinary chap who starts out on an ordinary day's activities and gets involved with other people's lives . . . the show depends from week to week entirely on what those other people are like.'

Written by Peter Tinniswood and David Nobbs (of Reggie Perrin fame), the series only lasted six shows. Sadly, the format didn't work, as Nobbs explains: 'The series was very misconceived although Peter and I didn't realize it at the time. The producer wanted Lance to work without the help of any other regular characters. That works with a genius, such as someone in the Chaplin mould, but it didn't with Lance. He's a very good actor but the show did him no favours at all. It was entirely the wrong way to go about it and we were too inexperienced to realize.'

'The producer wanted Lance to work without the help of any other regular characters. That works with a genius, such as someone in the Chaplin mould, but it didn't with Lance.'

Other memorable programmes from the period include *The Liver Birds*, which ran to eighty-seven episodes, including a revival in 1996. Carla Lane's sitcom about two young girls sharing a flat in Huskisson Street was a major success, as was Johnny Speight's *Till Death Us Do Part*.

Starring Warren Mitchell as Alf Garnett, the world's worst bigot, the sitcom's fifty-six episodes were shown between 1965 and 1975, spawning two revivals: *Till Death . . . a* six-part 1981 series for ATV, and the more successful *In Sickness and in Health*, which brought Garnett back to our screens for a further five series from 1985.

Garnett was a loud-mouthed, opinionated, expletive-spewing individual who berated his family for holding different views. With near-the-knuckle scripts confronting life's more controversial issues, Mitchell brought to life a character who'd earn himself a place in televisual history in a show that became a benchmark against which other sitcoms would be measured.

The character was conceived when Speight devised an aggressive socialist for *The Arthur Haynes Show*, before Garnett was later promoted to his own series as the head of a working-class family living in Wapping. Inevitably, the programme attracted more than its fair share of criticism from all quarters. In response to a Christmas episode, a minister from Liverpool claimed the programme must be 'offensive to many thousands of Christian people who treat the Christmas festival with the significance it deserves.' He added that, 'The dialogue was in every sense one of bad taste . . . the argument concerning the religious aspect of Christmas bordered on the blasphemous.'

A man from Wales, in 1968, said people in his country didn't subscribe to 'this low level of comedy'. He hoped that in future 'references to the Queen and the Royal Family, and also to the Prime Minister and Government, will be cut out, as this would not be allowed in any other country, and personally I do not consider these "jibes" as becoming to our country to which we are very proud to belong.'

One vicar went as far as attacking *Till Death Us Do Part* from the pulpit after the screening of the 1967 episode, 'Sex Before Marriage', asking his congregation to complain to the BBC and their MPs about the show. He claimed, reported the *Daily Sketch*, that the writer 'brings into our homes the smell of the sewers'.

In response to such complaints, the BBC's Head of Light Entertainment, Tom Sloan, drafted a letter which explained that 'comedy closely follows contemporary attitudes, and with shows like *Till Death Us Do Part*, we try to offer viewers an opportunity of seeing this exploratory kind of comedy.' Sloan's comments were backed up by favourable responses recorded in the audience surveys compiled by the Corporation.

After watching the pilot episode, on 22 July 1965, a member of the sample audience enthused: 'Oh, how delightfully vulgar. I laughed and laughed, yet in many ways it was all quite true to life.' It was a view echoed by nearly two-thirds of the people responding. A housewife commented: 'Hope this is a taste of things to come!' It was.

Other shows tickling the nation's funny bone during the sixties were *Me Mammy* (twenty-one episodes transmitted between 1969 and 1971), starring Milo O'Shea as high-flying executive Bunjy Kennefick, whose old-fashioned mother is forever ruining his plans; American show *Bewitched*, with the nose-twitching witch Samantha, played by Elizabeth Montgomery; *A World of His Own*, which ran for two series (1964-5), with Roy Kinnear playing the perpetual daydreamer who finds that such invigorating events as helping his wife (played by Anne Cunningham) to buy a new pair of shoes is enough to send him off into realms of fantasy; *Bootsie and Snudge*; ABC's *Those Two Fellers*, starring writers Sid Green and Dick Hills, who'd later write for *The Morecambe and Wise Show*, *All Gas and Gaiters* and *Sykes and a . . .* which saw Eric Sykes's long-standing working relationship with Hattie Jacques begin in earnest.

Spread over nine series, sixty episodes of *Sykes* were aired during the

BELOW: Tony Booth shares a Christmas moment with Warren Mitchell watched by Una Stubbs and Dandy Nichols in *Till Death Us Do Part*.

first half of the decade. The characters returned for an even longer outing (1972 to 1979) seven years later, this time in colour.

Over on ITV, Thames had a success on their hands with Johnnie Mortimer and Brian Cooke's *Father, Dear Father*. Over seven series, Patrick Cargill, as adventure writer Patrick Glover, found himself struggling to cope with life as a one-parent family, looking after two nubile daughters after his wife had run off with his best mate. Directed and produced by William G. Stewart, the series provided Patrick Cargill, already a leading man in theatre but less known on the small screen, with a show of his own. The writers had Cargill in mind when they began penning the series, and Stewart has nothing but fond memories of working with him. 'We knew we had a hit as soon as we did the pilot,' he says. 'And Patrick, who became a good friend, was easy to work with because he was a hard worker. He was meticulous at rehearsals and with the scripts, and if he saw a flaw in any part of the production, he was always prepared to mention it. He was a perfectionist.' One episode, titled 'Man About the House', and featuring a young Richard O'Sullivan, led to a series of the same name, which Mortimer and Cooke later wrote for Thames in the seventies.

Who can forget Granada's hugely successful series *The Dustbinmen*, written initially by Jack Rosenthal? Three series were made between 1969 and 1970, all stemming from a ninety-minute play, *There's a Hole in Your Dustbin, Delilah*, aired in 1968. The pilot was transmitted within a run of one-off dramas, but turned into a sitcom to good effect. Set in the coastal town of Fylde, the series followed the day-to-day adventures of a group of refuse collectors, played by actors such as Bryan Pringle, John Barrett and Trevor Bannister. Bannister's bin man was called Heavy Breathing. 'I loved the series,' says Bannister. 'I'll venture to say that it was the most extraordinary and amazing comedy series ever on British television, simply because it entered the *Guinness Book of World Records* for attaining the biggest audience viewing for any television comedy series. We had 21.5 million viewers for the first episode and maintained that throughout the first series.'

And, finally, the decade closed with the first of seven series from Ronald Wolfe and Ronald Chesney titled *On the Buses*. Back in those days, bus drivers weren't expected to be multi-skilled, having conductors to collect the passengers' fares. This left the main characters, Stan (the driver) and Jack (the conductor) with far more time to chat up the voluptuous clippies, eye up girls in miniskirts and torment their petty-minded boss, Inspector 'I 'ate you' Blake. While critics hated the show's bawdy humour, the public adored the innuendo-laden scripts, tuning in by the million to catch up with Stan, played by Reg Varney, and chirpy Jack, alias Bob Grant. Their official role in life was to drive the Number 11 bus, but, unofficially, they spent most of their time on more interesting pursuits. Seventy-six episodes were shown and, before long, it was one of the most popular shows on television. Its stars were treated as major celebrities. When Bob Grant married his third wife in 1971, the streets were so full of well-wishers that the newly-weds were forced to abandon their Rolls-Royce and make their way to the reception on foot.

BELOW: Reg Varney as Stan with Stephen Lewis playing Blakey in *On the Buses*.

THAT WAS THE WEEK THAT WAS

That Was The Week That Was has become something of a legend as a daring and ground-breaking late-night, satirical current affairs show. Although it is remembered as being sharp, witty and irreverent, *That Was The Week That Was* (thankfully, its title was commonly reduced to *TW3*) was the brainchild not of some darkly political television maverick, but of Hugh Carleton Greene – Director General of the BBC. It was Greene who decided that the BBC needed a show that would provide an alternative to the earnest, worthy and dangerously dull TV coverage of politics and current affairs. The man he chose to work out how this should be done was Ned Sherrin, then working as the producer of the early-evening current affairs magazine programme, *Tonight*.

Sherrin had a very good idea of how to go about assembling the sort of team he would need to produce a radically new style of show. While studying law at Oxford, Sherrin had put together a revue show called *Oxford Accents*, presented by the Experimental Theatre Company in association with the Oxford University Dramatic Society. The show was televised by the BBC in 1954 and Sherrin decided that his future most certainly lay in the world of entertainment rather than in the legal profession. Using the university revue style as his starting point, Sherrin crafted a format that was informal in its presentation, yet far from relaxed. It had the lively, almost frenetic pace of a student production, while also drafting in the steadfast social morality of the angry young men by spinning off from satirical comedy sketches into serious discussion on topical issues. Two pilot shows were made, with one of Sherrin's *Tonight* journalists, Brian Redhead, jointly hosting the first pilot alongside relative newcomer David Frost. While at Cambridge, Frost had been active with the Footlights Dramatic Club and had briefly been seen as a programme presenter on ITV before Ned Sherrin snapped him up for *TW3*. The second pilot was presented solely by Frost and when the programme was first broadcast on 24 November 1962, David Frost was the man fronting the show. *TW3* was to make Frost an international TV celebrity when he took over as host on the US version of the show in 1964 and it provided the springboard for an amazing career as a journalist, writer, film producer and television executive.

Along with its host, *TW3* featured an ensemble cast of huge talent, the regulars including Willie Rushton, Millicent Martin, Kenneth Cope, Roy Kinnear, David Kernan and Lance Percival. The show kicked off each week with Millicent Martin performing the theme song, the lyrics changing every episode to feature events in the news. Frost then led the viewers through a series of sketches and comedy performances, one regular item being Willie Rushton's far from flattering impersonation of Prime Minister Harold Macmillan. Legend has it that when the Postmaster General, Reginald Bevins (the man who granted broadcasting licences), said in an interview that he intended to do something about this mockery, he received a simple memo from Macmillan which read, 'Oh, no you won't.' Macmillan understood the power of television and knew that *TW3* kept him in the public eye while probably inflicting no more real injury to his career than that of a satirical political cartoon. One who almost sustained a very real injury on the show was Bernard Levin, the newspaper columnist, who regularly conducted interviews on the show and participated in the often heated studio discussions. During one live broadcast, he was attacked by a man from the studio audience whose girlfriend was an actress who had been the subject of a stinging review by Levin.

The studio audience was considered so important to maintaining the vitality of *TW3* that Sherrin decided there should be camera shots of the crowd. Not only that, but there were camera shots of other cameras, performers who were not at that moment 'on stage', overhead shots of the set and glimpses of the 'backstage' crew who would at that time never normally appear on a TV show. This all helped to involve the viewers at home, drawing them into the 'live' feel of *TW3*. And draw them in it did – to the tune of up to 11 million. By any standards that is an extremely impressive viewing figure for a show that was broadcast at 10.30 p.m. on a Saturday night.

Such was the nature of the show that it inspired many of those who watched it to pick up the phone and call the

BBC. Hundreds of calls were received during and after the broadcasts, and when the newspapers latched onto the fact that *TW3* callers were jamming the BBC switchboard, fans of the show who were concerned that the calls were all complaints also began phoning. Soon those who called to complain were being outnumbered by those who called with congratulations, some newspapers then opting to print a 'score', for and against, on Monday morning.

Although *TW3* ultimately ran to only two series, scores of writers provided material for the show, including Eric Sykes, Johnny Speight, Dennis Potter, David Nobbs, Bill Oddie, Jack Rosenthal, John Cleese, Malcolm Bradbury, Roald Dahl, Graham Chapman, Peter Cook, Michael Bentine and Richard Ingrams among many others. Despite

the quality of the writing and the show's undoubted popularity, however, the BBC took the decision not to broadcast it in 1964 as the corporation felt it needed to try to maintain its traditional image of impartiality during what was a General Election year. The last episode of *TW3* in the UK, a look back over the year featuring new sketches and highlights, was retitled *That Was The Year That Was* and broadcast on 23 December 1963.

BELOW: *TW3* regulars (clockwise) Millicent Martin, Ned Sherrin, Lance Percival, Willie Rushton, David Kernan, Kenneth Cope, Roy Kinnear, writer Al Mancini and David Frost.

SOAPS

Although the sixties had a fair sprinkling of soaps, the schedules weren't bubbling over with them to the extent they are today. Instead, TV executives understood the importance of soap operas in the overall picture and scheduled accordingly. Back then, instead of creating a soap-addict culture like that prevalent today, a wider range of televisual appetites was catered for, resulting in something for everyone on the box.

OPPOSITE: Angus Lennie and Noele Gordon in the *Crossroads* kitchen.

BELOW: The *Emergency – Ward 10* nurses included Jane Rossington (second right) who would later star in *Crossroads*.

As the years passed, competition between stations intensified, leading to a proliferation of soaps. Now, media attention is so intense that it often feels like we're being beaten repeatedly over the head with an ever-increasing supply of outlandish storylines; no longer, it seems, are we being prescribed a healthy dose of soap opera by the TV executives ruling our screen lives.

'Soap operas' – or, to give them the name under which they first developed, 'daytime serial dramas' – date back to US radio in the twenties when long-running drama serials were broadcast to an audience which, given that these were daytime broadcasts, mainly consisted of housewives. The radio advertising surrounding these shows was, therefore, predominantly aimed at the housewife, with cleaning products – soaps – proliferating. Unlike the stains the advertisements were promising to remove, however, the term 'soap opera' stuck fast as a collective name for this drama genre.

The first TV soap to be aired in Britain was *The Grove Family*, first broadcast on Friday 2 April 1954 at 7.50 p.m. on the BBC. There had, in fact, been an earlier children's series that could be termed a soap, *The Appleyards*, in 1952, but *The Grove Family* was the first of its type aimed at a mainstream audience. And the audience loved it. The show regularly

BELOW: Peter Bryant as Jack Grove at *The Grove Family* front gate.

pulled in 9 million viewers and the BBC was inundated with mail for the family. Broadcast live from the Lime Grove studios, from where the family around which the storylines revolved took their name, thousands of faithful viewers actually believed that Bob Grove and his family were real people. They even wrote in asking if Bob (a builder) could give them estimates for some building work.

British television saw the debut of a twice-weekly soap on 19 February 1957 when the first patients were treated in *Emergency – Ward 10*. Broadcast on Tuesdays and Fridays, the half-hour series was set in Oxbridge General Hospital, and pursued the private and public lives of the staff and patients. Starting out as a six-week drama titled *Calling Nurse Roberts,* the series quickly established itself, ultimately running for ten years and attaining viewing figures of up to 16 million on a regular basis, peaking with a phenomenal 24 million viewers.

One of the doyens of television soap is Richard Thorp, who's been playing *Emmerdale*'s Alan Turner for over two decades. 'I seem to have spent my life in soaps – I sort of foam when it rains!' he jokes. But it wasn't as part of a farming community that he began his love affair with the genre: he found fame after donning his doctor's coat, walking the hospital wards and causing many hearts to flutter as dashing Dr John Rennie in *Emergency – Ward 10*.

Initially broadcast live, there were inevitable calamities during the

ABOVE: *Emergency – Ward 10*'s Doctors Farmer and Mahler in TVs first interracial screen kiss.

making of the series, as Thorp recalls: 'In one episode my character was having a row with Glyn Owen's [Owen played Dr Patrick O'Meara]. We were meant to be storming through the ward shouting at each other. Reaching the end of the ward, we pushed open plastic swing doors, at which point the set fell down – but we just had to carry on! While we stood in the door frame continuing our row, I could see in the corner of my eye this actor, a famous drunk who loved playing patients in *Ward 10* because it meant he could lie in bed all day drinking. He'd been leaning against the wall and was now flat on the floor in his pyjamas clutching his bottle. The scene ended up with us absolutely shrieking at each other, desperately trying not to laugh.'

There was also an occasion when Thorp's dog made an unexpected appearance in the show. 'When the commercial breaks arrived, all that happened was that the studio would go into darkness for three minutes while everyone set up the next scene. Because there was no one at home to look after my dog, I had to bring it with me. As I prepared for the next scene, set in the common room, I handed the animal to a member of the crew, who turned out to be terrified of dogs. I walked on to the set, he dropped the lead and this enormous mastiff raced into the common room and sat down by my feet. In the end, a storyline was quickly written whereby a patient complained about a dog in the hospital – my dog got three episodes out of that.'

Such was the popularity of the show, created by ATV continuity writer Tessa Diamond, that fan mail poured in for the show's stars, particularly Thorp. 'There were masses of letters – it was almost like being one of the Beatles. If I went out, ladies would try and pull my clothes off. I must say, I thoroughly enjoyed that!' he says, smiling. 'For some strange reason they don't want to do it now. I think they're frightened of what they might expose.'

Reflecting on the success of *Ward 10*, Thorp says: 'Although there had been shows like *The Grove Family* before, *Ward 10* was the first proper soap. It was set in a hospital which, if you look at today's examples like *Casualty* and *Holby City*, is a popular setting. Everybody seems to like seeing other people cut up – and there's something very romantic about cuddling a nurse in her uniform!'

Romantic entanglements between Oxbridge General's staff members also led the show into what was, in the 1960s, a controversial area. In 1964 the show portrayed an interracial relationship between surgeon Louise Mahler, played by Joan Hooley, and Dr Giles Farmer (John White), which featured the first ever interracial on-screen kiss. Although rather tame compared to the love scenes we are used to seeing nowadays, the screen lovers were instructed to moderate their passion during the clinch to avoid accusations of it being too raunchy.

Thorp's character was deemed such a hit, especially with female fans, that a spin-off, *Call Oxbridge 2000*, sprang into life in 1961. 'It's hard to believe now, but I was quite pretty in those days,' jokes Thorp. 'They wanted to do something with my character so John Rennie moved out of the hospital and became a GP.' For an hour on Sundays, Thorp stepped into the shoes of Dr Rennie, a role he had enjoyed ever since arriving as a young casualty officer in *Emergency – Ward 10*. But if Thorp and everyone else associated with ATV's offshoot thought they would be enjoying the longevity of *Ward 10*, they were in for a big shock. Sadly, the Sunday slot did not pull in the viewers in the same way that *Ward 10*'s weekday screenings were doing and Thorp's life as a GP was short-lived. He was hanging up his stethoscope rather prematurely after just a year.

One of the first soaps to be spawned in the sixties and, arguably, the most influential British soap of all time, arrived on our screens in December 1960; it marked a turning point in the genre's development because here was a programme focusing on everyday problems experienced by a community of working-class characters. Within months, *Coronation Street* had an audience of over 20 million viewers tuning in for every episode. This came as a big surprise to some critics because it began life as a thirteen-part series that left reviewers so unimpressed that its premature demise was widely predicted. A journalist in the *Daily Mirror* wrote: 'The programme is doomed ... with its dreary signature tune and grim scenes of a row of terraced houses and smoking chimneys ...'

Set in a gloomy fictitious suburb of Manchester with, as the *Daily Mirror* noted, an equally gloomy signature tune, no one could have imagined how popular the programme would become. One of the show's strengths has been the endless

'...there's something very romantic about cuddling a nurse in her uniform!'

supply of memorable characters: who can forget Elsie Tanner, haughty Annie Walker or Ena Sharples, complete with hairnet?

Coronation Street was created by Tony Warren, who'd joined Granada Television in 1958, at the age of twenty-one. Initially working as a contract writer for producer Harry Elton, he cut his scriptwriting teeth on the detective serial, *Shadow Squad*, although he also contributed scripts to other shows. But he was desperate to write about a world he knew and, while he hadn't grown up in a locale like *Coronation Street*, Warren understood much about the kind of people living in such areas. As a nineteen-year-old unemployed actor, he'd penned a script spotlighting a northern back street, titled *Where No Birds Sing*. It never saw the light of day, of course, but the idea remained with him and when he was later asked by Elton to come up with an idea for a programme that would set the world alight, he based a script, titled *Florizel Street*, on *Where No Birds Sing*.

After writing a second script and an outline of the programme, executives at Granada gave it the thumbs up and both episodes were made, but the end product didn't excite the bosses. But for a stroke of enterprise by producer Harry Elton, it would have been curtains for *Florizel Street*. Positioning TV monitors around the studio, he invited a host of Granada employees, from cleaners to producers, to view the two episodes and record their feelings on a questionnaire. So fervent were the responses that in August 1960, sixteen episodes of Warren's creation were commissioned.

Just like today, much of the action centred around The Rovers Return, the local pub, where the first of many barmaids was Concepta Riley, played by Irish actress Doreen Keogh. She recalls: 'Tony Warren wanted an Irish barmaid and, as I'd just finished a successful play for Granada, I was asked to audition.' Intended to be pulling the pints for just three instalments, Keogh's character was serving the punters for four years, and, in 1962, was embroiled in an edge-of-the-seat storyline when Concepta's son, Christopher, was kidnapped. 'The viewing figures topped 21 million when the baby was kidnapped, which was amazing because not everyone owned a TV set then,' she says. 'But the enthusiasm of *The Street*'s viewers was extraordinary. Once I visited a pub with other members of the cast, and people were stripping the wallpaper for us to sign!'

Jennifer Moss was cast as Concepta Riley's eleven-year-old stepdaughter, Lucille Hewitt, and went on to play the character for fourteen years, though she never forgot her audition.

'I was fifteen but, being quite small, passed easily for eleven,' she remembers. 'In the audition scene I had to cry, which wasn't difficult because I was terrified! Lucille was fun to play because she did all the things I couldn't as a child. She had a tattoo, got involved with a hippy commune, looked after the gypsies – quite a rebel.'

Another essential part of daily life in *The Street* was the Corner Shop.

Two of its early owners were David Barlow, Ken's younger brother, played by Alan Rothwell, and Maggie Clegg, who was brought to life by actress Irene Sutcliffe. When David, a professional footballer, emigrated to Australia, where he was later killed in a car crash, Les, Maggie and Gordon Clegg moved in to run the store. Sutcliffe relived childhood memories of her parents' ironmonger's shop when she stood behind the counter of the Corner Shop. 'I often helped my parents so felt quite at home running the Corner Shop in *Coronation Street*. I had a smashing time on *The Street* – they were great days.'

Coronation Street was largely untroubled by competition for the first couple of years of its life, but then along came the BBC's *Compact*. Although never threatening the dominance of *The Street*, and panned by some critics, it became popular in its own right for the three years (1962 to 1965) it was shown, and within a month of being screened was attracting around 8 million viewers, increasing quickly to 12 million. It was the BBC's first serious foray into the genre since the demise of *The Grove Family*, back in the late fifties. Screened twice weekly, *Compact* told the inside story of a glossy women's magazine, focusing on the lives, rivalries and romances of the staff based at Enterprise House, the publication's HQ in London's Victoria. The *Radio Times* tried their best to whet their readers' appetite for the serial, stating: 'When a talented and temperamental group of men and women work together in the hothouse atmosphere of

BELOW: Television's most famous street-corner pub.

women's journalism, there's often far more drama – and romance – behind the scenes than between the covers of their magazine.'

Some of the employees during the publication's three-year screen life included Richard, the art director (played by Moray Watson); Joanne (Jean Harvey), the editor; Ian (Ronald Allen), who took over the editor's chair from Joanne; Alec (Leo Maguire), the staff photographer and Jimmy (Nicholas Selby), the features editor.

Compact was the brainchild of Hazel Adair (who had also worked on *Emergency – Ward 10*), writing the scripts with the help of Peter Ling, with whom she'd create *Crossroads* two years later. They formed a prolific writing partnership, with comparable writing styles just one of their attributes. They first collaborated on the children's show, *Whirligig*, before joining forces to write *Compact*. Although writing as many scripts as possible themselves, occasionally other scribes were drafted in to help, always guided by the duo's detailed story treatments. While ten weeks' worth of story outlines were maintained, scripts for seven weeks hence were required. This exacting task created pressure, as Adair explained to the *Radio Times* on 17 September 1964: 'It's true that we have to live

AROUND THE WORLD 1964

Beatlemania gripped America as the Liverpudlians crossed the Atlantic, meeting Cassius Clay (Muhammad Ali) along the way, while author Ian Fleming, creator and writer of the James Bond novels, died of a heart attack. By the time everyone settled down to eat their Christmas turkey and pull their crackers, MPs had decided to scrap the death penalty for murder, Radio Caroline had become the first pirate radio station, conflict between Mods and Rockers had brought chaos to seaside towns and the BBC had launched its second channel.

almost in each other's pockets . . . we both have big families to occupy our off-duty time, so there's small chance of any personal friction. Even so, getting out *Compact* calls for real discipline, so we both keep strict office hours.'

The serial was conceived while Adair was visiting the BBC to discuss another project with Eric Maschwitz, the Head of Light Entertainment. He told her that he was considering a new twice-weekly show for prime time and wondered if she had any ideas. Never one to say 'no', Adair described her magazine-based idea and he requested an outline without delay. 'I'd had an idea about a women's magazine for a while but was considering writing it up as a play,' she explains.

> 'The BBC were keen to adopt a realistic documentary style but we felt that wasn't the objective at all: it was the content that grabbed the viewers and the fact the show attracted the highest rating of any BBC programme at the time proved our point.'

Realizing the series, if commissioned, would involve plenty of work, she invited Peter Ling to co-write the series. Over a weekend they devised a format, developed storylines and agreed on a working title of *The World of Eve*. Having written for women's magazines, Adair was familiar with the day-to-day workings of a publication. 'The BBC were keen to adopt a realistic documentary style but we felt that wasn't the objective at all: it was the content that grabbed the viewers and the fact the show attracted the highest rating of any BBC programme at the time proved our point.'

After the first two episodes, 'The First Edition' and 'Advice to Readers', had been screened on Tuesday 2 January and Thursday 4 January 1962, the BBC's Audience Research Department conducted a survey of viewers' opinions. While some felt 'the idea had very little to commend it', the majority liked what they saw and hoped the serial would establish itself. Eric Maschwitz, reflecting on the report's findings, wrote: 'I am not so depressed by those viewers who dismiss the project from the start as encouraged by what seems to be the "wait and see" attitude of others.'

The programme, which initially had a £1,500 budget per episode, was soon grabbed by the Drama Department, but attempts to make its storylines more earnest were resisted by Adair and Ling. 'The show had a humour – we sent ourselves up,' says Adair. 'It was always light-hearted: after all, it was devised as light entertainment.'

Whatever category it was allocated, by September 1962, Eric Maschwitz was lauding the success of *Compact* and the general idea of screening a twice-weekly serial in a prime-time slot. In a memo to the Assistant Controller of Programmes, he mentioned that the success of *Coronation*

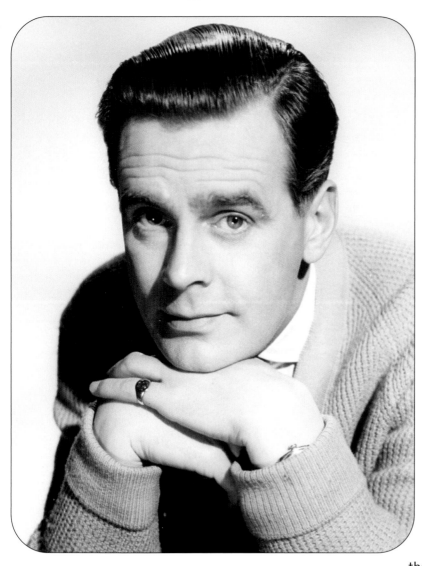

Street and *Compact* had even 'turned the thoughts of TV executives on the other side of the Atlantic to the possibility of "soap operas" being as successful in prime time over there.' He added that: 'The other network [ITV] has devoted a great deal of time, thought and money to the development of further series of this kind. This is particularly true in the case of ATV – with *Emergency – Ward 10* losing freshness and audience in opposition to *Compact*. They are not finding the task easy, the reason for this being in my view that the right background for a twice-weekly serial is very difficult to discover.'

An unusual element of the series was an interview with a well-known personality – starting with actor Ian Carmichael – which was integrated into the storyline. The personalities appeared as themselves, being interviewed for the magazine. In the beginning, Hazel Adair was the interviewer.

When Adair and Ling turned their attention to their next hit, *Crossroads*, the workload intensified and, while retaining control of the *Compact* storylines, other writers were hired to complete the scripts. Eventually, after nearly 400 instalments, the printing presses ground to a halt at the *Compact* offices and the last edition of the programme was aired. Adair was understandably disappointed with the Beeb's decision to drop the show. '*Compact* had given me an enormous amount of pleasure – I loved the whole thing. But the BBC always seemed a bit wary of success in those days.'

Despite lauding *Compact* for its initial popularity, it was only nine months into the show's life before Eric Maschwitz was considering a successor. Writing to Donald Baverstock, the then Assistant Controller of Programmes (Television) in September 1962, he mentioned that to date he had received two suggestions: *Small Film Unit* and *Australian Family in*

Britain, neither of which enthused him. He added: 'Since then, North Region has offered a pilot for a series entitled *This Young World*, a poor effort, though I paid them the compliment of telling them to "go away and think again".'

Maschwitz had subsequently spoken to other writers, three of whom suggested ideas. Talbot Rothwell, who wrote the lion's share of the *Carry On* scripts, came up with *Chadwick Three*, based on life in a London County Council tower block, while two other scribes offered an idea based on life in London during the Second World War. All were held in abeyance, together with *Office Block*, an idea formulated by Donald Baverstock himself. Nonetheless, it was clear Maschwitz had reached the conclusion that, albeit popular, *Compact* would never topple ITV's successful *Coronation Street,* and he wanted to seek out alternatives that might fare better against commercial television's ratings winner.

While the BBC decided on a successor to *Compact*, a twice-weekly serial titled *199 Park Lane* turned into an adequate stop-gap. During the eighteen episodes, shown over a nine-week period, viewers dropped in on the residents of a plush London apartment block – bankers, politicians, film producers, couturiers and gossip columnist Tony Asham (played by Philip Bond) – who seemed to spend most of their social time partying. Written by William Fairchild, whose credits included screenplays for the war films *Morning Departure* and *Malta Story*, as well as the 1931 picture, *Passage Home*, fans of the recently finished *Compact* were able to find solace in the fact that the new soap featured some familiar faces: Brenda Kaye, who'd played sophisticated fashion editor Lorna Willis-Ede in *Compact*, and Henry Gilbert, Mr Magnum in the former show, both joined the *199 Park Lane* team.

When the short-lived soap – branded 'false, stale and hateful' by Frederick Laws in the *Listener* in August 1965, and having endured a 'short, unhappy life', in the eyes of Adrian Mitchell in the *Sun* in October 1965 – disappeared quietly without trace, two new soaps, *The Newcomers* and *United!*, were introduced to the schedules. Originally regarded as competing programmes, battling it out to succeed *Compact* as the Corporation's primary soap, they ultimately ended up running concurrently as stand-alone projects. In July 1965, however, the Beeb's drama booking manager, John Henderson, issued a memo titled '*United!* versus *The Newcomers*'. Both series came with an option date, and Henderson pointed out that 'the decision about which serial goes into gear has got to be made before the seventeenth'.

First to be commissioned was *The Newcomers*. Created and written by Colin Morris, this soap, which ran between 1965 and 1969, followed the trials and tribulations of the Cooper family as they adapted to life in a

FOR GREEN-FINGERED VIEWERS

The advent of colour television on BBC2 in 1967 made the world of difference to garden lovers. Now, instead of watching Percy Thrower extolling the virtues of his black-and-white dahlias and marigolds, we were able to see his display in brilliant colour. The long-running show *Gardeners' World* bloomed in 1969, taking over the mantle of the BBC's premier gardening show from *Gardening Club*, also presented by Thrower, who quickly became TV's first celebrity gardener. Whereas *Gardening Club* was studio-based, with microphones stuffed in soil to help pick up the presenter's voice, *Gardeners' World*, which is still going strong today, invited viewers into Thrower's own one-and-a-half acre plot just outside Shrewsbury, as well as visiting gardens open to the public. If you were more interested in fruit and veg, though, you had to wait until the programme was transmitted from Clacks Farm, where Arthur Billitt, an old chum of Thrower's, set aside land specially for the Beeb. Thrower was a crucial influence in altering people's perception of gardening, showing that it could be therapeutic and not all about toiling away up to your knees in mud.

'new' country town, the fictitious Angleton. The move was instigated when Arthur Huntley, the managing director of Eden Brothers, manufacturers of electrical components, decided to relocate the company to a sleepy town in East Anglia. Inevitably, this led to a host of challenges and adjustments for its workers, including Ellis Cooper, foreman of the winding shop. Original producer Verity Lambert felt the show's realism, stemming from the talents of creator and writer Colin Morris, was what attracted its audience.

'Colin had written some powerful drama documentaries, says Lambert. 'He wasn't afraid to deal with difficult subjects, such as prostitution; he explored real-life situations and was probably the father of drama documentary. I didn't stay with the show for long, but enjoyed being involved in it – you felt part of a situation that people were having to deal with in their everyday lives. Consequently, a programme focusing on such issues possessed a resonance of reality about it.'

Writing responsibilities were initially shared between Morris, who'd conceived the idea, and Australian writer and producer Anthony Coburn. They met in April 1965 to discuss the twice-weekly serial's format. Compiling a report afterwards, Coburn pointed out that when it came to agreeing the setting for the programme, they both reacted against 'some smoky, dour, bleak, northern industrial town'. He added: 'We feel we might be typical of many viewers who have had a bellyful of the north and the Midlands and that if our serial is to have any freshness and originality, these things would stand a better chance of growing in some area which in television terms is virtually unexplored.' Morris and Coburn thought of East Anglia and, in particular, King's Lynn.

While *The Newcomers* established a loyal audience – although never ground-breaking in terms of viewing figures, with no more than 5 million people tuning in each episode – it received a mixed reaction from the press. When the *Daily Sketch*'s TV critic, Shaun Usher, criticized the show, readers wrote in, classing his comments as 'harsh'. One lady from London, disagreeing with Usher, wrote: 'This serial, which thank goodness avoids sex and violence, is most refreshing, clean and an interesting story of decent family life.' Another reader from the capital added: 'Mr Usher should remember that even if he doesn't like *The Newcomers*, some people are tired after a day's work and need light entertainment to relax.'

Meanwhile, writing in the *Sun*, journalist Adrian Mitchell was upbeat about the show. Noting that the 'BBC's serial trouble over the past six months makes cheerless reading', he felt that 'now it is paying off in the form of *The Newcomers*, which has lasted and sounded good since episode one.' He acknowledged that some might feel the show was covering 'prosaic, well-trodden ground', but challenged that view, explaining: 'We have had plenty of family melodramas and domestic tittle-tattle – but very little domestic drama.' Examining its qualities, he observed: 'In its quiet way it talks about social problems and manages to make very good jokes about people without degrading them.'

In the Midlands, the regular column 'Jay's Say' in the *Birmingham Evening Mail*, dated October 1965, was enamoured of the show, reporting: 'To my mind this is not only by far the best of current serials on either channel, but perhaps the best yet seen since Marconi.' Despite applauding the new serial, Jay had just one grumble, believing the soap was over-earnest towards the 'social problems and the social divisions inherent in the transplanting of factory workers from London to a rural area'.

Before the end of its first year, Huw Weldon, then Controller of Programmes (Television), wrote to everyone involved in the programme congratulating them on the impressive start. In his memo, dated 5 November, he wrote: '. . . because it really does seem to me that *The Newcomers* has all the signs of a very distinguished serial, I thought I might just as well say so . . . I could wish that the figures were better

BELOW: Alan Browning starred as Ellis Cooper in *The Newcomers*.

already. But I would not wish for the serial not to be as good. The fact of the matter is that I admire it. It seems to me to be extremely well written so far, much better written than most serials that I see.'

Sadly, the programme's faithful audience never grew to the size expected by BBC hierarchy. The show also suffered, as far as many viewers were concerned, when key cast members left, most notably Ellis Cooper (played by Alan Browning) and Vivienne Cooper (Maggie Fitzgibbon). This was highlighted by members of the sample audience questioned by the BBC after the screening of the final episode, on 13 November 1969. Although most were saddened by the Beeb's decision to scrap the show, many felt the departure of some of the original characters had 'lessened its attraction'. One person remarked: 'The biggest mistake was letting Maggie Fitzgibbon leave', while others stated the new characters introduced to the serial failed to live up to the standard of the Coopers. A woman summarized the general reaction, saying: 'When this series started I wouldn't miss an episode if I could help it, but gradually all the good characters were faded out . . . I can say I have enjoyed it but lately it has gone a bit tame.'

Even though ITV's *Footballers' Wives* has been a runaway success in our own time, few dramas, soaps or comedies over the years have centred around events on and off a football field. Yet the BBC, soon after launching *The Newcomers*, maintained their drive to succeed in the world of soaps by throwing *United!* into the schedules as competition for its commercial opponents. With former player/manager-turned-TV-presenter Jimmy Hill installed as football advisor on the twice-weekly serial, *United!* followed the fortunes of Brentwich United, a fictitious club struggling in the Second Division doldrums. For this serial, originally envisaged as a drama series, Anthony Cornish, a radio producer at BBC Birmingham, teamed up with former art teacher-turned-scriptwriter Brian Hayles to create a show concentrating, initially, on the relationships within a football club. The scope was widened to appeal to more than just soccer fans, with local grounds, including Birmingham City's and Coventry City's, utilized for action sequences.

The series kicked off with actor David Lodge playing Gerry Barford, Brentwich's newly-appointed manager, striving to return the club to the big time. Of course, life is never easy in soapland and his path to success was hampered by internal squabbles and myriad issues, including inciting jealousy amongst his players by picking his son for the team.

The show's journey was a rocky one, and within six months a major upheaval saw seven regular characters axed and a raft of new writers brought in to pep up storylines. But *United!* ultimately failed to strike the right balance between on-the-field action and off-the-field drama. After three years of attracting little more than 6 million viewers, full time was blown on life at Brentwich United in 1967.

Soaps are often easy prey for world-weary critics, but no programme in the genre, it would seem, has been the target of such negative and vituperative criticism as *Crossroads*. By the time the last edition of their earlier creation, *Compact*, was aired, Hazel Adair and Peter Ling had their scriptwriting teeth well and truly stuck into the Midlands-based soap, and day-to-day events at the country's most famous motel had become a staple part of life for millions of viewers.

> 'We didn't cover the whole of the country for some time. When the London region finally started receiving it, we had to do a special production with Meg Richardson talking to the camera explaining the story so far, to establish who she was and how they came to be there.'

Some critics said the acting was as unstable as the scenery, but no one could question the show's popularity. The viewing public were soon addicted to Meg Richardson, wheelchair-bound Sandy, unreliable Amy Turtle and the rest of the motley crew. Thousands of episodes were shown between 1964 and 1988, and the public's unquenchable thirst for all things *Crossroads* was extraordinary.

The show began when Lew Grade, who ran ATV, decided that he wanted to launch a half-hour daily serial. He had received one idea from a writer and, while discussing another project with Hazel Adair in his office, he asked if she'd read the proposal and report back. Although she liked the idea, Adair felt it lacked depth for a daily serial. After calling her regular writing partner, Peter Ling, they sat down during a weekend to formulate their own plans for a show, which Lew Grade wanted as a vehicle for actress Noele Gordon. They presented their idea and awaited Grade's verdict. 'He read our three or four pages of storyline ideas and character profiles, pumped his cigar and said: "OK, we'll do yours",' Adair remembers, adding that the meagre budget caused headaches for the writers. 'The budget was even more pitiful than what we had on *Compact*, which we were still writing at the time, of course. We had £750 per programme. Everything, including the cast and our fees had to come out of that. All Lew Grade provided was the studio and the technicians. We couldn't do half the good ideas we'd come up with because there simply wasn't the budget.'

The initial working title of *The Midland Road*, due to its supposed location between Birmingham and Stratford-upon-Avon, soon changed.

'I'd always thought of the letter "C" as being lucky. We'd had the success of *Compact* and four of my children's names begin with "C",' explains Adair, 'so we came up with *Crossroads*. There was always a motel but it was set at a crossroads, hence the name.' The basic premise revolved around Meg Richardson (played by Noele Gordon), a mother-of-two who couldn't afford to run the family home when her husband died. Upon hearing a motorway was being built through her land, she took full advantage by converting her house into a motel.

For millions, teatime wouldn't have been the same without the regular trip to the Crossroads Motel, but initially the programme was shown in only a few regions, as Peter Ling explains. 'We didn't cover the whole of the country for some time. When the London region finally started receiving it, we had to do a special production with Meg Richardson talking to the camera explaining the story so far, to establish who she was and how they came to be there.'

The most talked about motel in history was set in King's Oak, a fictional village in the Midlands. Running to over 4,500 episodes, *Crossroads* became a legend of the genre, despite continual scathing attacks from the press. Part of its appeal was a unique charm, an element the recent short-lived revivals were unable to recreate. Cherished by a faithful following, *Crossroads* quickly became the subject of endless wisecracks. Tony Adams, who first played estate agent Mr Perkins in 1968, before, a decade on, playing wily accountant Adam Chance, recalls: 'Critics used to say the programme was as exciting as watching paint dry.'

Catching up with motel gossip became addictive for viewers. All right, the scenery may have wobbled and characters vanished for months without trace, but fans weren't concerned

BELOW: Noele Gordon headed the *Crossroads* cast as Meg Richardson.

because the show's foibles were part of its charm. This may help to explain why, at its peak, audiences of more than 17 million were commonplace. Peter Ling feels much of the criticism from papers was unjust, particularly as the soap developed. 'Whereas on tape you can stop, rewind and redo things or simply edit, the programmes were on film where there really is no chance to do any editing. They were recorded as if they were going out live and went out without any form of editing. If something like the scenery fell down, the only thing you could do was go back to the beginning and start the whole episode again. Because of that, lots of things that later on would have been edited out, actually went out on screen, and this is why people always talked about actors forgetting their lines and so on.'

Like other examples of the genre, *Crossroads* had its share of major storylines that also became headlines. Some of the stories were, believe it or not, way ahead of their time. Lynette McMorrough, alias frumpy waitress Glenda Brownlow, became something of a pioneer in soapland when her character had a test-tube baby, played by her real-life daughter, Emily. 'In many ways, it was forward-looking, particularly with the storylines it tackled. I have nothing but good memories of playing Glenda, despite the fact she was always moaning and her life was full of doom and gloom.'

BELOW: Jane Rossington, Ronald Allen and Sue Lloyd by the famous *Crossroads* sign in 1982.

MILESTONES AT *CROSSROADS*

1964 The motel receives its first guests

1965 Amy Turtle appears on the scene, initially working in a general store

1966 'Miss Diane' (Diane Parker) joins as a waitress

1967 A wartime bomb explodes beneath the motel, killing one of the cooks

1968 Tony Adams's first appearance in *Crossroads* – but as Mr Perkins, an estate agent, not Adam Chance, who wasn't seen until 1978

1970 Meg adopts a black girl, Melanie Harper, and David Hunter invests in the motel. Becomes general manager a year later

1972 Sandy is crippled after a car crash

1974 Eccentric chef Shughie McFee takes over the kitchen

1975 Benny first seen, working on a farm. Amy Turtle jets off to America

1976 Glenda is raped

1979 Meg's hubby, Hugh, dies of a heart attack while being held by kidnappers

1981 The motel burns down on Bonfire Night

1983 Adam and Jill marry

1988 The end of the road. The then owner Tommy Lancaster puts the hotel up for sale. Jill heads off into the sunset with John Maddingham to buy a small hotel in the West Country

The show also featured a rape story. To ensure the storyline was as realistic as possible, advice was sought from Birmingham police regarding the way rape victims were treated and how the matter was handled.

'As well as being a sensational storyline, we tried to make sure people learnt more about the whole subject,' says Peter Ling, who recalls the moment he realized just how important *Crossroads* was to its viewers. 'My daughter, then a teenager, always sneered at the programme. One day, we were on the pier at Hastings, in one of the amusement arcades. The woman giving change for the machines said: "Excuse me, are you Peter Ling?" When I confirmed I was, she replied: "I've been watching *Crossroads* ever since it began." She was a spinster, all her family had died and she lived alone. She added: "At the end of the day I go home, make myself a cup of tea and some supper, switch on the set and watch *Crossroads* – the characters have become my family. I live through them, really." That's what she did every day. When my daughter and I left the pier, [my daughter] said: "I'll never laugh at the programme again." It made her realize that some people found it terribly important in their lives.'

Despite Lynette McMorrough's own character falling foul of the show's legendary lapses in continuity (Glenda went off to the loo and wasn't seen for seven months), she feels critics were overly harsh. 'Some journalists were very scathing about particular actors and always wanted to knock the show.'

CROSSROADS – WHERE ARE THEY NOW?

NOELE GORDON (Meg Richardson)

The face of *Crossroads*, she earned the nickname 'The Godmother' from fellow cast members. Sacked in 1981 when the producers attempted to give the show a new look, she died in 1985, aged sixty-one.

SUE LLOYD (Barbara Brady)

A model before turning to acting, she was married to actor Ronald Allen in real life. Gave up acting in the mid-1990s to concentrate on a painting career.

TONY ADAMS (Adam Chance)

Quit in 1987, days before learning the show was to be dropped. Reprised his role in the latest revival. Remains busy on stage.

JANE ROSSINGTON (Jill Harvey)

Stepped back into Jill's shoes for the recent revival. Popped up in *Brookside* a few years back but nowadays most of her work is on the stage.

PAUL HENRY (Benny Hawkins)

Has experienced his fair share of heartache since hanging up Benny's green, woolly hat. His teenage daughter was killed by a drunk driver and he was involved in several failed business ventures. Recently appeared in the prison drama, *Bad Girls*.

Behind the Crossroads reception desk rather than behind the camera, one of the production team discusses the script with Sue Lloyd, Ronald Allen, Sandor Elès and Jane Rossington.

RONALD ALLEN

(David Hunter)

Moved to America after playing smoothie David Hunter. Married Sue Lloyd in 1991, by which time he was suffering from cancer. Died in 1991.

ROGER TONGE

(Sandy Richardson)

Worked for the Post Office when offered the role of Sandy. Died of cancer in 1981.

ANN GEORGE

(Amy Turtle)

Dropped in 1975 but made the occasional appearance in the 1980s. She died of cancer in 1989, aged eighty-six.

ANGUS LENNIE

(Shughie McFee)

Still acting. One of his more recent jobs was playing Badger in *Monarch of the Glen*.

SANDOR ELÈS

(Paul Ross)

Played haughty head waiter Paul Ross for four years. The Hungarian-born actor experienced financial hardship in the final years of his life. Died of a heart attack in 2002, aged sixty-six.

Noele, Gordon, Ronald Allen, Jane Rossington,
Paul Henry and Richard Tonge pose for a publicity shot.

A target for regular criticism was motel cleaner Amy Turtle, brought to life by Ann George. The worst gossipmonger this side of Spaghetti Junction, she was rarely spotted without her obligatory duster, lurking in the shadows in order to be in earshot of people's conversations. And let's not forget that she became the focus of one of the programme's most bizarre storylines, when old Amy was accused by a foreign guest of being a former KGB spy – plots don't come any better than that!

Because Ann George would occasionally forget her lines, they were scrawled all over the back of the beer mats she turned over while dusting the bar, but there was precious little respite elsewhere from the pressure of producing the daily soap. Exacting deadlines and lack of editing facilities, particularly at the start of the show's run, meant that it wasn't just actors fluffing lines that caused directors to pull their hair out in frustration – temperamental props didn't help, either. The motel's resident chef for eight years, Angus Lennie, will never forget his encounter with a carving knife. Briefed on how best to slice a cucumber, Lennie reached for the knife and filming began, but it wasn't long before things went wrong. 'Everything seemed fine until I looked down and saw blood everywhere,' smiles Lennie.

One of the soap's most famous faces was Jane Rossington, who played Jill Harvey; she appeared in the opening scene, back in 1964, uttering those immortal words, 'Crossroads Motel, may I help you?' She, too, recalls many hiccups during filming. 'I was in a scene talking to Stan [Jill's husband at the time] when suddenly the sponge cover came off the microphone above our heads and fell on the floor between us. I casually picked it up, put it in my handbag, and carried on.

'It wasn't that the production team didn't want to do any editing to delete such mishaps, it's just that it wasn't allowed for in the budget – simple as that; we also didn't have time. We completed each show as if it were live, starting at scene one and working through until the end. There were forty-five minutes to film each show on tele-cine, so you could start again if something went terribly wrong at the beginning, but after that whatever happened, happened.'

This explains why, when Amy Turtle walked out of shot and fell over while carrying a tray, she was totally ignored by the other actors in the scene who simply gritted their teeth and carried on, despite the clatter of glasses off-camera. 'There were no editing facilities for some years, which is why the programme got its dreadful reputation for sets wobbling,' explains Rossington. 'Considering the pressures we were under, I think we did awfully well.'

Rossington recalls having plenty of fun on the programme, although terrific tension usually existed in the studio. 'I remember we did a dinner party scene which was a nightmare. Nowadays a director will never use

AROUND THE WORLD

1965

While millions of Brits were soaking up the sun on their summer vacations, one American was taking the idea of adventure holidays to the extreme by becoming the first US astronaut to walk in space, although he was not the first man to do so. Russian cosmonaut Alexei Leonov made the first space walk a few months earlier. What the American astronaut, Ed White, achieved by venturing out of his capsule for fourteen minutes was to spend four minutes longer floating around than Leonov had done. Meanwhile, Winston Churchill died, US marines entered Vietnam and The Beatles were awarded the MBE.

more than one camera, but we had four. The characters in the scene, including me, were sitting and couldn't lean forwards or backwards because we'd be moving into someone else's shot. We were almost at the edge of hysteria, just waiting for it to go terribly wrong. Eventually we reached the end of the scene, after which they cut away to the next sequence, being filmed just twenty yards away. In the euphoria that we'd got through our scene correctly, the actor sitting opposite me got up, turned and walked straight into the set. All the pictures fell off the wall: it was out of shot, but there was a terrific crash. We'd got through this horrendous scene only for that to happen.

'But things like that occurred often and we'd all be lying on the floor trying not to laugh, like the time I was in a scene doing something at a sink. The cameraman was shooting over the sink, and up until that point we didn't have running water. When it came to the take the supply was switched on but I suddenly realized I'd pulled the plug out and there was no bucket underneath. Water was gushing everywhere but we just carried on.'

Rossington, who made a brief return in Carlton's ill-fated revival of the series, stayed with the soap through its twenty-four-year life. Not bad considering she was originally told the job would run for just six weeks. 'I'd been in *Emergency – Ward 10* before going off into rep at York to do a play. The same casting director who'd hired me in *Ward 10* was casting *Crossroads* and remembered that I came from the Midlands.'

She attended an audition, during which her shopping bag split and tins of baked beans rolled across the floor. Jane still got the part, of course, and it couldn't have happened at a more fortuitous moment. 'The chap employing me in rep wasn't paying my full salary. I kept saying: "I'm a bit short." I was getting cross so when *Crossroads* came up it was a good chance to say: "I don't care now because I'm going off to do something else."'

As a character, Jill didn't have the most exciting of storylines to begin with, but Rossington was pleased with the way she matured. 'It was a young girl-next-door type of role, so there wasn't much to do, but the character got better and became much more fun. I had some very nice light comedy material, particularly towards the latter days.' Rossington admits that she's surprised the show lasted as long as it did. 'Everyone always seemed to be against it. We had so many enemies in the industry that I'm amazed we survived so long.'

Like the millions of fans, most of the cast hold fond memories of *Crossroads*. Tony Adams says: 'My character, Adam, changed from week to week, sometimes alarmingly. Part of the fun of the programme, though, was that anything could happen, and invariably did!'

The cast became experts in disguising the unexpected glitches: in one scene, Noele Gordon should have been pouring tea but played the entire scene standing against a safe door which kept swinging open.

The show underwent several makeovers during its lifetime, including the motel being transformed into a country hotel, but by the mid-1980s it was struggling to attract the younger viewers who could secure its long-term future. On 4 April 1988, the final episode – or so everybody thought – was screened. Recently, two attempts to revive the soap have failed dismally. Some would argue that the modern versions weren't given enough time to establish themselves, but in today's cut–throat industry, time is a priceless commodity.

Who can recall Anglia Television's answer to *The Archers*? That is how some critics labelled *Weavers Green*, the soap set in a fictional East Anglian village of the same name. Beginning in 1966, each of the forty-nine half-hour episodes centred on a rural veterinary practice run by the Armstrong family, and were written by husband-and-wife team, Peter and Betty Lambda, creators of the programme. Although the show ran twice weekly, on Thursdays and Saturdays or Sundays, depending on where you lived in the UK, it was never given the chance to settle into a regular slot where it could attract a substantial following. As former actress Betty Lambda confirms, 'It didn't work. We'd have liked the programme to be shown either during the week or at weekends, but not a mixture of both because back then it was a different audience who watched television at weekends.'

Nevertheless, Anglia struggled to resolve the scheduling issue over the weekend edition and pulled the plug after little more than a year. The Lambdas were dismayed, especially as they learnt about their soap's plight in the press. 'We were at home and my husband came into the kitchen and said: "*Weavers Green* is dead!" He'd read it in the paper.'

Kate O'Mara, who played the young vet, 'Mick' Armstrong, was equally disappointed when the show stopped. 'It was successful, but the network refused to give it a regular slot so people couldn't get into it. I spent most of my time on horseback, and that's not me because I'm the world's worst horsewoman. I also found myself with my hands up cows' interiors and things like that, so it was a very broadening experience.'

ABOVE: Kate O'Mara played a young vet in *Weaver's Green* in 1966.

Like all long-running shows, there were times when things didn't go as planned. Kate recalls a scene involving a cheetah, hired from a circus. 'I had this animal on the end of a chain, but it didn't like filming. It suddenly roared and pulled on the chain. His keeper, who was hiding in the bushes, was whispering: "All right, Cleo, calm down, Cleo." I thought: "Don't worry about Cleo, what about me?" I heard him say, "Keep going," so I carried on dutifully, even though I was terrified.

'When I completed the scene I couldn't believe it – because the camera crew had disappeared, they'd run for their lives which meant I'd done it all for nothing. Then, when we got [the cheetah] into the studio, it hated the lights and attacked its keeper, swiping its paw across the man's forehead, drawing blood in the process.'

If you're finding *Weavers Green* difficult to recall, then perhaps you remember *Market in Honey Lane*? It was the sixties answer to *EastEnders*,

although it was produced by ATV instead of the Beeb and lasted two years
not two decades. Running between 1967 and 1969, it was, like *EastEnders*,
made at the Elstree Studios and centred on an East London street market.
London's Honey Lane had, in real life, been the site of a market between
the mid-seventeenth and early-eighteenth centuries. Although created
and written by Louis Marks, it was his wife, who'd lived above a street
market in Soho, who suggested he write a programme based around such
a location. Storylines centred upon the traders and customers whose lives
revolved around the market, characters brought to life by, among others,
John Bennett, Michael Golden, Ray Lonnen, Vicki Woolf, Pat Nye and Anna
Wing, who'd later reappear as Lou Beale in *EastEnders*.

For John Bennett, it put his name on the television map. 'It made me
very well known and, even after all these years, older people still
remember me from that show. The principal characters were all
stallholders, with my character, Billy Bush, selling aubergines, avocados
and courgettes.

'I chose those because they were the only things they couldn't get as
plastic replicas. Therefore, they had to buy them fresh and at the end of
each show, I'd take a box of avocados home.'

Beginning life as a fifty-minute single-drama evening show, it attracted
much praise when it was launched. Journalist Peter Knight reported that
Associated Television had built a full-scale market outside the Elstree
Studios, adding: 'The same care and regard for authenticity have also been

LIGHT ENTERTAINMENT

Television companies group all sorts of shows under the 'light entertainment' banner. During the sixties there were more shows that obviously fitted the light entertainment mould; programmes that were clearly developed from the theatre world's variety format. One such show was *Sunday Night at the London Palladium*.

First broadcast in 1955 with Tommy Trinder as host, the live show was a huge hit but rose dramatically in the ratings when a new compere took over in 1958, the young Bruce Forsyth. Brucie swiftly took the viewing figures up beyond 14 million, although during its heyday in the 1960s the show would boast 28 million viewers – half of the entire population tuned in. *Sunday Night at the London Palladium* always started in the same way, with the Tiller Girls dance troupe high-kicking their way across the stage. The host (Forsyth gave way to Norman Vaughan in 1962, who was followed by Jimmy Tarbuck from 1965-7) then introduced acts such as comedians, jugglers, magicians or singers before the trademark game show 'Beat The Clock' brought the first half to a close. The second half featured a further few acts before the top-of-the-bill star rounded off the evening. All of the performers then appeared for a final curtain call, smiling and waving from the Palladium's famous revolving stage. A few refused to take this final bow – the Rolling Stones, for example, felt that it just wasn't cool.

Morecambe and Wise, on the other hand, were delighted to appear on the revolving floor and did so a dozen times in 1960 before ITV gave them their own show in 1961. The double act had endured less successful forays into television in the 1950s, but the new ITV show was to see them crowned Kings of Light Entertainment. Their variety formula of sketches, guest artists and musical numbers made them the country's best-loved comedy act and they stayed with ITV until 1968, when they switched allegiance to the BBC, then the only UK service broadcasting in colour. They were to remain with the BBC for the next ten years.

Comedy was an essential element in any light entertainment package and comedians like Benny Hill, Tommy Cooper, Frankie Howerd and Mike and Bernie Winters all appeared on screen throughout the sixties with their own versions of the old variety formula. By 1969, however, shows like *That Was The Week That Was* (actually produced by the BBC's Current Affairs rather than Light Entertainment department), Spike Milligan's eccentric *Q* series and 1967's *At Last the 1948 Show*, inspired the creation of a programme that would change the nature of TV comedy forever. The first series of *Monty Python's Flying Circus* began in October 1969, running to January 1970 and ushering in a new era of comedy for the seventies.

ABOVE: The Beatles appeared with Eric and Ernie on *The Morecambe and Wise Show* at Christmas in 1963.

> ‘*Market in Honey Lane* has the seeds of decay in it, like a barrer-boy’s tomato.’

given to the script and characters if last night’s first episode is anything to go by.’ Fellow critic Peter Black gave an equally generous appraisal: in May 1967 he claimed it had the potential to be ‘up there with *Z Cars*’. A month earlier in the *Sun*, Nancy Banks-Smith warned that the programme had the ‘seeds of decay in it, like a barrer-boy’s tomato’, and if great care were not taken it could ‘slide into soft-centred sentiment’. She did, however, heap praise on actor John Bennett and writer Louis Marks, saying that they acted and wrote ‘as if they were next-door neighbours’.

The programme was later retitled *Honey Lane*, adopting a style more associated with soaps. It eventually lost its prime-time slot and was shunted into a twice-weekly afternoon position, replacing the short-lived *Driveway*, which drove off into the sunset after just sixteen episodes. Commissioned by Lew Grade at ATV, *Driveway* followed the fortunes of Major Alan Brock, played by Anthony Newlands, and everyone associated with the driving school he ran.

Playing Shirley Pickering, an instructor, was actress Marjie Lawrence, who regarded it as a departure from most other studio-bound productions. She says: ‘Most of the action centred around the driving instruction and the interplay between me as the instructor and the characters being taught. Village life was bound up in the storylines, so there was much involvement with local characters.

‘The cast and crew got on famously – it was a very happy unit. There was never any pressure. In the sixties, plenty of time was allocated for rehearsals and this resulted in each episode being completed on schedule. It went on for sixteen glorious weeks. The series got good ratings, but had been scheduled only for that short run. Then it was squeezed out by a number of previously booked programmes, so we all lost out.’

ATV really milked the soap scene in the sixties, with another of their crop, *Harpers West One*, appearing in 1961. Created and written by the prolific duo, John Whitney and Geoffrey Bellman, the show ran until 1963, with thirty-two hour-long episodes transporting us into the world of high street fashion. The series was set in Harpers, a large London department store. The staff included receptionist Susan Sullivan, played by nineteen-year-old Wendy Richard. Running high in the TV ratings throughout a significant part of its screen life, the serial was the result of ATV founder Lew Grade’s search for a contemporary-based show that would engage viewers from day one.

As John Whitney explains, a shop setting seemed ideal. ‘Department stores had a relevance: most people, wherever they lived, had visited large stores. It was a nice canvas on which to paint characters, which led to so many stories to be told. Every element of that store provided stories, whether it was pilfering of goods, people passing themselves off as important people to obtain other services or complaints. Even now, I could think up thirty storylines without too much trouble.'

And before Kevin Laffan created *Emmerdale Farm* in 1972, he was writing about the residents of two large Victorian houses that had been converted into unfurnished flats in a Yorkshire coastal town, supposedly near Whitby. Yorkshire Television's *Castle Haven* ran for only a year (1969 to 1970), but during its short life the tenants seemed to experience more than their fair share of problems and heartache. Now largely forgotten, the show featured some names we've come to associate with soapland, including Gretchen Franklin and Jill Summers, as well as Roy Barraclough and Kathy Staff as Harry and Lorna Everitt. Barraclough feels Yorkshire's first attempt at a soap was hyped up so much that it was always going to be difficult to live up to expectations. 'It was classed as a big competitor to *Coronation Street*, so immediately Granada refused to take it, as well as another region who were well in with Granada. It was only shown in a few regions.' But the show was beset with other problems – a few episodes into the run, the local transmitter collapsed and disrupted the soap's transmission for several days.

Barraclough enjoyed his short spell as Harry Everitt. 'The storylines weren't cutting edge, more cosy, including in-fighting between the residents of the flats. Harry and Lorna Everitt had two rowdy young kids. We were the terrible, noisy neighbours living on the ground floor – very low-life people,' he says, smiling. 'But I look back on the show with great fondness, partly because it kick-started my television career. Up until then, I'd done bits and bobs, including a couple of small roles in *Coronation Street*, but this was my first running part in a television series.'

If you were resident in Scotland during the sixties, chances are you caught one of the 200-plus instalments of another soap set in a block of flats. *High Living* began in 1969 and was set in a Glasgow high-rise. If *Castle Haven* has slipped quietly from the public conscience, this soap has disappeared even further into the mists of time.

BELOW: Wendy Richard worked in Harpers long before she had a job at Grace Brothers.

SIXTIES' QUIZ & GAME SHOWS

Often seen as schedule fillers by critics, the longevity of television quiz and game shows, despite them normally being dumped in a mid-afternoon graveyard slot, speaks volumes for the genre's popularity. Of course, back in the sixties, contestants would be lucky to win a fiver. Nothing, however, diminished the British fascination with answering questions or laughing at everyday people making fools of themselves on the latest game show.

Although not the most ingenious of formats, quiz show *Pit Your Wits* built up a loyal following. Launched on the Beeb in 1962, it had originally started out as *Pencil and Paper* on commercial television before its producer and creator, John Irwin, was persuaded to jump ship and bring the show to the BBC. Shaw Taylor had presented the ITV show but it was Kenneth Kendall, who'd decided to quit reading the news to establish a wider remit of work, and Gwynneth Tighe who presented the BBC show.

Reflecting on *Pit Your Wits*, Kendall recalls: 'John Irwin was very keen on audience participation. There were no prizes on offer and, in a way, the show was terribly amateur and old-fashioned compared to what you see nowadays. Gwynneth and I sat side by side on a sofa with a sheet of questions, taking it in turns to ask the viewers questions.' It was as simple as that. At the end of the programme viewers were given the answers and told how well they had done based on their scores. The programme's rudimentary style was just what John Irwin wanted. He told the *Radio Times* in 1963, on the eve of a new series: 'There is nothing whatever – no flashing signs, no spinning wheels, no revolving scoreboards – to distract attention from the job in hand. We are even cutting out competing teams in the studio, so that viewers can have it all to themselves.'

A year before the BBC gave us *Pit Your Wits*, Granada provided a young presenter called Bob Holness, later to achieve cult status as the presenter of *Blockbusters*, with his first taste of a major network programme on *Take a Letter*. Holness recalls how Granada gave him his start in TV: 'I'd come over from South Africa, where I'd been working on radio, and was offered a contract by Granada. I stayed with them seven years, employed as a factotum – doing everything from bit parts and commentaries to reading news bulletins and presenting jobs.

'It was the best apprenticeship you could have because I did everything and anything that came along. *Take a Letter*, which was like a television crossword, was moderately successful, and saw a team of two competing in each game. It was probably a bit too serious for its own good, but nevertheless ran for two to three years.'

If you were feeling particularly brainy, you could join Bamber Gascoigne on *University Challenge* to test your knowledge against the long-haired – or short-haired in the case of one Stephen Fry who made his TV debut on the show while at Cambridge – university students taking part. In its original guise, this ever-popular show originally ran from 1962 to 1987. A format bought from the US, where it began as a radio show titled *College Bowl*, it underwent very few changes when Granada screened it. Gascoigne was producer Barrie Heads' first choice. 'We tested a few people and Gascoigne was by far the best. He was then writing drama criticism for the *Spectator* and I liked his style as a writer, so I just thought I'd try him. He was outstandingly good in the auditions. He was very relaxed, extremely fluent and had a good personality. He used to research the questions and made sure he knew the subjects so that if there was any doubt he could explain the answer himself.'

One of the show's memorable features was the split screen, which mystified many viewers for years; they believed the teams were, in fact, seated on top of one another. Beginning with the Universities of Leeds and Reading battling it out, the show became an immediate favourite.

Another favourite, featuring 'Bernie the Bolt' shooting at apples each week, was *The Golden Shot*. In the grand finale a blindfolded cameraman was guided through the aiming and firing of a telebow (a crossbow tied to a camera) by a telephone contestant. Various hosts presented the show during its seven-year run, including Norman Vaughan, Charlie Williams and, most famously, Bob Monkhouse.

But many people's favourite face on the show was that of Anne Aston (opposite), the ever-cheerful hostess, who helped to inject humour into the show. Anne, whose real surname is Lloyd, smiled her way through six years (1969 to 1975) of the hugely popular teatime show, endearing herself to viewers when caught on camera counting contestants' scores on her fingers. Her popularity spawned a cartoon character in girls' magazine, *Jinty*, and saw comedians Mike Yarwood, Freddie Starr and Benny Hill impersonating her in their shows. Now in her fifties, she recalls: 'I was working in the family travel business when I read in the local paper that *The Golden Shot* was moving from Elstree to be made at the Aston studios in Birmingham. I loved the show and wrote asking if they'd need anyone. I was shocked when invited to audition and then offered a job. When I tried registering with Equity, the actors' union, I discovered there was already a member called Anne Lloyd, so ended up being named after the television studios.

'I have great memories of the programme. I worked with three different presenters on the show, including Bob Monkhouse, who was lovely. He was kind, considerate and always wanted me to do well. Some comedians you work with want all the laughs, but he wasn't like that.

'A lot was made of me calculating the scores on my fingers, which became something of a gimmick. I was adding up the scores when I suddenly realized I was being watched by 16 million people. My memory went blank and I ended up counting on my fingers. Everyone laughed so much we made it part of the show, with me fumbling with my numbers, making it appear a real effort.'

Being live TV, lots of things went wrong, including a couple of the contestants going missing in the studio. 'I couldn't find them anywhere so had to bring on a couple of stand-ins instead, which fooled Bob Monkhouse because he was expecting different names. The real contestants were finally found in the canteen. I also remember slipping and falling over while going to read the scores. Being live meant everyone saw it.'

Seeing people make fools of themselves is always good for a laugh, and ideal material for a television series, which explains why *It's a Knockout!* became such a phenomenon. Presented by David Vine and Stuart Hall over the years, who can forget Mr Hall's uncontrollable laughter in response to the mayhem unfolding before him, or Mr Rugby League, alias Eddie Waring, as referee?

The contest, which was adopted by European broadcasters as *Jeux Sans Frontières* (Games Without Boundaries), grew out of a British show from the 1950s. *Top Town* was an inter-town talent contest which became so popular it soon attracted the attention of the French, who sent two producers across to watch the show being made. Before long, they were staging their own competition, but with a difference: *Interville* became a knockabout competition, which the *Radio Times*, in 1967, referred to as a 'battle of skill in a series of bizarre contests like outdoor party games'. Its success spawned a Europe-wide show, and in 1967 Britain took part for the first time. As the years passed, the events became ever more bizarre, like the time four men with sledgehammers took part in a piano-smashing race, aiming to shatter the instrument into pieces small enough to post through a letterbox. Sounds great fun!

The Daleks threatened
to take over the universe
armed only with a sink
plunger and an egg
whisk in *Doctor Who*.

SCI-FI & ADVENTURE

The sixties was the space-race era. With the USSR and United States battling it out to be first to send a man into space, to have him walk on the moon and to explore the mysteries of the solar system, it wasn't surprising that programme makers cashed in on this tide of space-age fervour. Such exciting advancements, culminating in American astronaut Neil Armstrong setting foot on the lunar surface in 1969, led to a plethora of sci-fi shows on television. There was still plenty of atmosphere here on Earth, however, as the televisual battle against crime raged ever more fiercely. There were so many TV shows about elite branches of crime-fighting organizations, each enjoying a 100 per cent success rate, that it's surprising there were any criminals still roaming the streets.

BELOW: Roger Moore loved *The Saint*'s Volvo so much he bought his own and still drives a Volvo today.

The sixties marked the peak of this genre of programming. Certainly, special effects were, at times, laughable compared to today's standards, but the production line was kept busy churning out a steady supply of shows, many now regarded as cult classics. Save for a few examples, including the recently revived *Doctor Who*, these series are seldom seen on TV today. The only chance for the modern generations of kids and teenagers to experience shows such as *Department S*, *The Champions* or *The Avengers* is via the DVDs and videos of those who became hooked on them the first time round and couldn't resist buying the tapes and discs in a moment of nostalgia.

The rebirth of *Doctor Who* must surely have evoked powerful memories for those old enough to have watched the series in the sixties. I wonder if anyone reading this chapter will admit to being one of those kids who was so frightened watching the Doctor on Saturday evenings that they took refuge behind the sofa? For many, the haunting screech of the theme tune set the mood perfectly and it wasn't long before the show became a 'must-see' programme. It's hard to believe that *Doctor Who* didn't set out to be a sci-fi series. Sydney Newman, BBC's Head of Drama in 1963, was looking for something to fill a gap in the schedules between *Grandstand* and the music show *Jukebox Jury*. He opted for a programme he saw as both educational and historical – it was only later that it was regarded as science fiction.

Original producer, Verity Lambert, says: 'It was loosely based on H. G. Wells's *The Time Machine*; kids are more particular as viewers, they don't get fooled as much as adults do, so I wasn't going to talk down to them in any way, and that was the pith of it, really.'

The first Doctor embarking on intergalactic adventures was played by movie veteran William Hartnell. Lambert had seen him playing some key roles. 'He played a hectoring sergeant-major in Granada's *The Army Game* and this rather sad loser in *This Sporting Life*. His performances confirmed he had the ability to be scary, which Doctor Who was supposed to be, while other times vulnerable. He was my favourite Doctor because I cast him – but he was superb.'

Lambert was also aware of his ability to play tough, military types, something he'd done regularly on the big screen. 'That was another aspect I liked,' she admits. 'You didn't want someone who was a pussy cat, you needed someone who had some edge and could be quite dangerous because the character would find himself in some drastic situations – often as a result of his obstinacy.'

The Doctor's journeys were always beset with problems, many posed by his arch-enemies, the Daleks, who made their debut in 1963 in the second story of series one. Just like the Doctor's time machine, the TARDIS (originally intended to be able to adopt an appearance relevant to the

OPPOSITE: William Hartnell confronts some unconvincing aliens in *Doctor Who*.

ABOVE: The Doctor first came across the Cybermen at the South Pole in 1966.

period to which it had travelled, before budget limitations put paid to the idea and it was stuck as a police box), the Daleks became an integral part of the show's success. The germ of the idea was planted in writer Terry Nation's mind after watching the Georgian State Dancers.

'It was a performance about chess people, and it was watching these pieces glide across the stage which got him thinking,' says Lambert.

The responsibility for turning Nation's idea into reality fell to Raymond Cusick. As production designer, his remit covered sets and props, but as the show was bereft of a special-effects designer, Cusick became involved in creating the sinister Daleks, too.

'I spoke to the writer, Terry Nation, and we both agreed it shouldn't be a man in a suit, which was being suggested at the time for cheapness because budgets were tight,' says Cusick. 'I realized the operator inside would have to be in the studio all day and would need to be seated, so I started drawing a chair.

'I then simply drew a shape around the operator, with the top part louvred with black gauze inside so he could see out but no one could look in. The bottom of the Dalek was open and the operator, wearing plimsolls, simply pushed it along. They were made of fibreglass and I wanted them to be smaller than the average human being, so I made them just 5 feet 3 inches tall.'

As no one expected the Daleks to become a long-term enemy of the Doctor, only four were constructed; whenever crowd scenes necessitated the appearance of other Daleks, six full-length photos were utilized to give the impression others were lurking in the background. When the first seven-part Dalek adventure ended in February 1964, producer Verity Lambert, believing the creatures had served their purpose, donated two to the Dr Barnardo's Homes (as it was then called) children's charity organization, while placing the other pair in storage. But when the Beeb was inundated with letters from anxious viewers demanding more Dalek stories, she had to rescue those she'd discarded.

Veteran Dalek operator, Cy Town, who joined the team during the Jon Pertwee era, confirms pushing Daleks around was tiring work.

'Sometimes in the studio, especially if you were tearing up and down corridors, it could get hot, but on location, which always seemed to be a sandpit in Devon, it was quite cosy,' he recalls. 'I played other monsters over the years, involving masks and tight costumes, and they were much more uncomfortable than being a Dalek.'

Moving the castor-mounted creature required the operator to push it along. This sounds straightforward enough, but when the castors were substituted with a ball-like mechanism supposedly to aid in the negotiation of difficult terrain on location, disaster was never far away.

THE DOCTOR'S MOST DEADLY RIVALS

As well as the infamous Daleks, the Doctor has had to battle against some gruesome-looking foes. Were you frightened by any of the following?

THE SONTARANS Bellicose, egg-headed creatures, first seen on twelfth-century Earth in 1973.

THE GIANT SPIDERS Crept into view in 1974. They imprisoned their enemies before slowly devouring them.

THE ICE WARRIORS Cold killers who first appeared in 1967. They had sonic weapons attached to their arms.

THE CYBERMEN These mechanized monsters arrived in 1966 when the TARDIS landed at the South Pole.

THE DOCTOR'S WHO'S WHO

The changing face of *Doctor Who* is perhaps one of the reasons the show has enjoyed such a long life, with each individual helping to retain a freshness by embellishing the character with his own idiosyncrasies. But can you remember all the actors who've portrayed the time-travelling Doctor? Well, here they are . . .

WILLIAM HARTNELL (1963-6: three-and-a-half series, including the pilot) A veteran film actor, he was an apprentice jockey before turning to acting. Died, aged sixty-seven, in 1975.

PETER CUSHING (1965-6: two feature films) Horror-movie specialist Peter Cushing played the Doctor in two films, *Doctor Who and the Daleks* (1965) and *Daleks: Invasion Earth 2150 A.D.* (1966). He died in 1994, aged eighty-one.

PATRICK TROUGHTON (1966-9: three series) Made his small-screen debut in a 1947 TV version of *Hamlet* and appeared in his first two movies in 1948, one of which was again *Hamlet* and the other *Escape*, which also starred William Hartnell. Died, aged sixty-seven, in 1987.

JON PERTWEE (1970-4: five series) Popular radio actor in *The Navy Lark*, Pertwee scored another TV hit playing the colourful scarecrow, Worzel Gummidge. Died, aged seventy-six, in 1996.

TOM BAKER (1974-81: seven series) Tom Baker clocked up most appearances as Doctor Who. Since then, he's worked extensively on stage and screen, including playing Donald MacDonald in *Monarch of the Glen* and providing the narrator's voice in *Little Britain,* as well as writing a bestselling autobiography, *Who on Earth is Tom Baker?* in 1997.

PETER DAVISON (1982-4: three series) Well known for his time in vet series *All Creatures Great and Small*, Davison's recent small-screen credits include *At Home with the Braithwaites, The Last Detective* and *Distant Shores*.

COLIN BAKER (1984-6: three series) Worked as a solicitor before acting. Since *Doctor Who*, Baker has been busy on stage, including playing the Doctor.

SYLVESTER McCOY (1986-7: three series) Started acting under the name Kent Smith. Other TV work includes *Frank Stubbs Promotes* and *Rab C. Nesbitt.*

PAUL McGANN (1996: one TV movie) Best remembered for his debut in the cult movie, *Withnail and I,* his other work includes appearing in TV's *The Monocled Mutineer* and *Hornblower.*

CHRISTOPHER ECCLESTON (2005: one series) Became the ninth BBC incarnation of *Doctor Who* when the Beeb revived the series, but then shocked his bosses by announcing he wouldn't stay for another series. The latest Doctor has now been confirmed as David Tennant.

BELOW: Richard Hurndall played William Hartnell in 'The Five Doctors' and a dummy played Tom Baker at the publicity shoot.

'They kept falling off and limited our movement,' says Town. 'In one story you'll see a Dalek doing a three-point turn for the first time.' For the 1973 episode, 'Death to the Daleks' – staged yet again in a sandpit – the Daleks were assembled on a mini-railway track. 'We came hurtling round the bend and one of the Daleks toppled over. Luckily, no one was hurt.'

Restricted vision caused havoc, too, especially when having to manoeuvre through doors. 'I remember one scene saw a procession of them coming out of a spaceship and it was really tight,' recalls Town. 'All you could hear was "Bang, Bang" as we all tried to get through!'

Perhaps more than any other genre in television, sci-fi and adventure shows called upon the services of stuntmen. With this dependency on visual effects, people like Derek Ware, one of the industry's best-known experts, were regularly in demand. During his long career, Ware has worked on hundreds of films and television shows, and even formed his own company, HAVOC, supplying stuntmen for the big and small screen. He recalls his experiences of working on *Doctor Who*: 'My initial fight arrangement came in the first adventure and was between two pre-historic tribesmen in a cave. Surprisingly, the BBC agreed to have stuntmen substituting for the actors who'd been cast, so I doubled Jeremy Young and Billy Cornelius subbed for Derek Newark. The result was very realistic and came in for quite a bit of criticism from parents – but not from kids!

> 'We came hurtling round the bend and one of the Daleks toppled over. Luckily, no one was hurt.'

'For the next decade I devised fights and stunts for the series working with three different Doctors – William Hartnell, Patrick Troughton and Jon Pertwee. Jon was the most adventurous as he could ski, swim, handle a motorboat and motorbike and had raced at Brooklands Motor Course before the war. He was prepared to do all his own stunts and acquitted himself well considering he was in early middle age and suffered a recurring back problem.'

Ware explains that his 'funniest experience' on *Doctor Who* was during the 1966 story, 'The Smugglers'. 'I was asked to supply a stuntman to play "The Spaniard", a rival to the "Pirate King", who was required to do a lot of swinging on ropes, flourishing a sword, and uttering bravura dialogue such as: "The men are sick of you, Captain Blackheart, and I'm taking over this ship!" I racked my brains for someone who could speak lines and look like Errol Flynn. Imagine my surprise when I was told the part was mine.

'I learned all the lines and practised all the speeches, only to be asked on the first day's filming: "Haven't you got the rewritten script?" I was then issued one, which read: "Enter 'The Spaniard', a short, ugly, deaf mute, cunning and vicious – not a man to turn your back on"!'

AROUND THE WORLD   1966

A month after Gemini 9, an unmanned American spacecraft, had landed on the moon in June, the whole of England rejoiced as the national football team lifted the World Cup at Wembley, beating West Germany 4-2 in extra time. The year, though, ended on a sad note as legendary cartoonist, Walt Disney, died aged sixty-five. There was tragedy for the Welsh mining village of Aberfan, when a slag heap engulfed the tiny community killing 144 people – more than 100 of them children.

In 1962, year before William Hartnell ventured forth in his old police box, ABC aired a sci-fi anthology series titled *Out of This World*. Introduced each week by Boris Karloff, who became synonymous with horror roles after playing Frankenstein, it was so well received that when Sydney Newman jumped ship to become the new head of the Beeb's drama department (hastily preparing itself for a substantial increase in output with the impending launch of BBC2), he revisited the format and *Out of the Unknown* was born. An anthology series of science fiction stories, the show ran to four series between 1965 and 1971 and was initially produced by Irene Shubik, who had worked with Newman at ABC on *Out of This World*. Shubik had seen *The Twilight Zone* in America and when she joined Sydney Newman's team at ABC in the UK, she started hunting for sci-fi stories: 'I didn't want the bug-eyed-monster-type stories, rather something with a philosophical or sociological thesis, so I began with John Wyndham [best known for *The Day of the Triffids*] and various people in that category.' Original screenplays and adaptations of classic stories from the genre were used to great effect in *Out of This World*.

When Shubik later joined Newman ready for the launch of BBC2, they developed the *Out of This World* concept to create *Out of the Unknown*, which comprised not just of sci-fi but included mysteries, too, with plays like 'A Desirable Property', 'Somewhere Nearer Home' and 'The Girl from Sicily'. Meanwhile, E. M. Forster's 'The Machine Stops', dramatized by Kenneth Cavander and Clive Donner and addressing a frightening prediction about Man's future in a machine age, won first prize at the Trieste Festival for sci-fi films in the summer of 1967. But the series kicked off with an adaptation of a John Wyndham story. 'No Place Like Earth' was set on Venus and Mars, depicting life for a homesick earthling stranded on Mars after the Earth explodes. Terence Morgan played the lead, supported by, among others, Hannah Gordon.

Just like *Out of the Unknown*, many other shows in the sixties exploited the public's fascination with time travel. In *The Time Tunnel*, James Darren, as Dr Anthony Newman, and Robert Colbert, as Dr Doug Phillips, were determined young physicists who dedicated themselves to proving the feasibility of time travel – the trouble was, they eventually got lost in their own creation, and were seen at the beginning of each episode tumbling along a time tunnel. The American series, reputed to be the most expensive on American television in 1966, failed to live up to expectations and was kicked into space after just one season.

The theme of travelling through time was popular with writers and producers because it afforded the opportunity to exploit their own imagination. Although not strictly a time traveller because he didn't intentionally set out to transcend the decades, crime-fighting Edwardian Adam Adamant found himself incarcerated in ice by his arch-enemy before waking up six decades later. Twenty-nine episodes of *Adam Adamant Lives!* were spread over two series during 1966 and 1967, and regarded by many as the Beeb's answer to *The Avengers*, perhaps because Sydney Newman was instrumental in creating both shows.

So why did the dashing exponent of law and order end up encased in ice? Predictably, it was down to love. Tricked by his two-timing girlfriend, Louise, who faked her own kidnapping, Adamant tore off to rescue his beloved, only to be captured by his greatest adversary, The Face. He injected our hero with an eternal-life drug and Adamant lived on in a state of suspended animation until he finally escaped from his frozen living death in 1966, when a demolition gang inadvertently blew open his ice mausoleum. Adamant quickly became involved in the crime-fighting world when another girl – will he never learn? – Georgina Jones, ran into trouble.

Given the job of producing the series was Verity Lambert, whose busy career had most recently included *The Newcomers* and, of course, *Doctor Who*. 'I'd been producing *Doctor Who* for about eighteen months and wanted a change. I asked Sydney [Newman] if I could produce *Adam Adamant Lives!* I thought it was a wonderful idea, although not a new one in terms of having someone observing another time.'

Lambert knew Gerald Harper was ideally suited to the lead role. 'I'd seen him in some classical piece and thought him perfect for Adam Adamant: the way he looked, his voice – there was something about him.'

In a memo dated 20 August 1965, she provided colleagues at the BBC with an outline of the new series and its central characters. Of Adamant she wrote: 'This is a man who is highly intelligent and extremely well educated. He has been to public school and has university degrees in several subjects . . . He is superb physically, and is able to handle any kind of weapon expertly. His attitudes are those of the Victorian era, i.e. he is fiercely patriotic, believes in the Empire, he respects women and he always behaves like a gentleman towards them. He dresses elegantly in Edwardian style and his speech is always strictly from that period.'

Harper was invited to meet Sydney Newman and Verity Lambert to discuss the show, which was scheduled to replace *The Man from UNCLE*, but for a while it seemed as if the Beeb would be looking elsewhere for their leading man.

Harper recalls: 'After they explained the idea to me, I replied: "That's wonderful, but I'm afraid you'll have to count me out because I've already agreed to do a play on Broadway."'

Facing a major setback, Newman asked Harper to leave the room.

'I went outside and sat next to his secretary for about ten minutes.' says Harper. 'They then called me back in and said: "Look, we're going to offer you the part of Adam Adamant. We want you to know this will make you immediately famous throughout the land – it's too important for you not to do it. There's the phone: will you please ring the producer and ask him to release you?" I rang and he very kindly agreed, which was lucky because the show opened on Broadway, had three previews and then closed!'

Playing hip sixties' girl, Georgina Jones, alongside Harper was Juliet Harmer, although the role was played by Ann Holloway in the pilot episode. Harmer, meanwhile, had only recently qualified as a children's teacher at Cambridge. 'I was completely amazed to be offered the job. When I was at Cambridge, I'd taken part in various university revues; the thing I most loved was how theatre completely merged the social differences between people, and at this point I began secretly to aspire to a career beyond teaching, maybe in children's television.'

> '. . . he is fiercely patriotic, believes in the empire, he respects women and he always behaves like a gentleman . . .'

Harmer, who now concentrates on painting as well as writing and illustrating children's books, says: 'I always thought of it as much as a situation comedy of manners as it was a sort of detective/sci-fi series. I was very lucky: I'd done a stint in children's and schools' television, a couple of episodes of *The Avengers*, a short film that had won a prize at Cannes, and various commercials. So I had done very little, yet it was all good experience, working with good directors.'

Gerald Harper recalls that it didn't take long to attract the viewing public's attention, with the opening episode watched by nearly 11 million. 'It became successful very quickly. After just six weeks I heard Frankie Howerd making jokes about *Adam Adamant* on the radio. I thought: "If it's become something that national figures make jokes about, you know it's caught the public's imagination."'

Harper was warned that the show would make him a household name. A week before the first episode was transmitted, he was dining with one of the writers. 'He said: "Do you realize that two months from now you won't be able to walk down the street without being talked about and recognized?" For about fifteen or twenty years he was absolutely right.'

Playing Adamant – full name Adam Llewellyn de Vere Adamant – generated plenty of fan mail. 'In those days, I had an enormous amount of hair. Sydney Newman had this bee in his bonnet that I should have a widow's peak, so they built this hugely expensive and beautiful wig which I wore throughout the series, even though I had my own hair underneath.

'One day I was in Richmond Park riding a horse and all the young girls from a nearby ballet school were out dancing and giggling. As I rode

ABOVE: Gerald Harper in *Adam Adamant Lives!* with Juliet Harmer playing his girlfriend Georgina Jones.

'I thought, "Oh my God, he's going to get up and kill me."'

quietly past I heard one of them say in a heartfelt way: "Hasn't he got lovely hair!" It was the only bit of me that wasn't mine.'

Much was made of Adamant's physique and his prowess as an athlete, including his fencing skills. Derek Ware, a stunt coordinator on the series, confirms that Harper was ideal for the role. 'As the hero carried a sword-stick at all times, this was his first line of defence, and Gerald Harper was no slouch when it came to cut and thrust. In fact he did most of his own action and did it well.'

One scene saw Harper fighting Nosher Powell, a heavyweight boxer before he became a stuntman. Harper remembers Powell paying him a flattering compliment: 'In three days' rehearsal you don't have time to learn the lines and certainly don't have time to learn how to fight well. He said: "Listen, Gerald, you can handle it. You just try and hang on and I'll look after myself, all right?" Of course, the adrenalin flowed and I caught him with the most ferocious left hook you've ever seen, and he went down. There was stunned silence.

'I thought, "Oh my God, he's going to get up and kill me." Fortunately, he got up, rubbed his chin and said: "You've got a bloody good punch there, Gerry." He never laid a glove on me once, which I thought was very generous.'

Producer Verity Lambert initially described the series as an 'action-adventure series, with humour arising from a sidelong glance at life today'. Early episodes received a lukewarm reception by critics. The *Daily Express*'s James Thomas wrote that Harper played Adamant with a 'splendid tongue-in-cheek bravado' but noted that it was a 'shame that the bulk of the audience which would appreciate Adamant is in bed.' Over at the *Daily Telegraph*, Norman Hare commented: 'It is all right for the BBC to have a little fun occasionally, but whether last night's joke called *Adam Adamant Lives!* can be sustained for the next fifteen Thursday evenings is very doubtful indeed.' He closed his article with a stark warning: 'Unless it shows some improvements, this series is going to be one of the biggest flops the BBC have ever had on their hands.' Peter Black, writing for the *Sunday Times*, said: 'Gerald Harper's Adam had little chance to establish the charm without which such characters must sink. And this goes for Juliet Harmer's Georgie.'

But some critics were more positive, with the *Daily Mirror*'s Ken Irwin classing the central character as 'one to watch'. He added: 'There is an intriguing originality about this dandy character but, somehow, he remains dreadfully square. Adam is the best comic character the BBC has produced in a long time.'

And it wasn't just journalists giving the programme the thumbs down. When the BBC compiled an internal Audience Research Report after the screening of the opening episode, viewers were frank, too. The report's compiler quoted one viewer, who said: 'Now I shall be able to attend to the garden on Thursdays as well as Mondays', before confirming that such 'disgust' was 'evidently shared by a good many viewers in the sample, who found this first episode . . . far-fetched and ridiculous in the extreme.' Another viewer remarked: 'Ham from start to finish. A disastrous follow-on in the *UNCLE* spot. As far as I'm concerned, the sooner Adam Adamant ceases to live, the better!'

Although the show attracted a loyal band of followers, it didn't live up to the BBC's expectations and audience figures gradually dropped, as confirmed by Sydney Newman, when he wrote to Gerald Harper at the end of the second series. Full of praise in his letter dated 10 April 1967, he said: 'I thought you were absolutely marvellous and if the series didn't have quite the long life we had hoped it would have, this had nothing to do with you, or in fact Juliet or Jack [May]. This series, from where I sat, was a near miss – we were so close to really having something great, but somehow or other it just eluded us.'

Gerald Harper's career wasn't affected by the demise of *Adam Adamant Lives!* and shortly after he was offered the lead role in *Hadleigh*, a character who emerged from a series titled *Gazette*. Reflecting on *Adamant*'s failure to get into gear, he says: 'It was a brilliant idea but the only problem was that it was rushed. We did one episode every week for thirteen weeks, which nowadays would be considered madness. It was almost as if it was a stopgap.'

In hindsight, producer Verity Lambert felt she never managed to find the ideal writer for the series, but dismisses claims that it was the BBC's answer to *The Avengers*. 'A lot of skilled writers used to write for shows like *The Avengers* and they were very witty and clever – but it was a different kind of wit. I never managed to find the people who

BELOW: Patrick Macnee as John Steed with Honor Blackman as Cathy Gale in *The Avengers*.

> '**We never got the right tone and I became frustrated with the series because it fell short. Even a lot of writers thought of it as** *The Avengers.*'

could provide the kind of clever, witty scripts I was looking for – what I really wanted was a Mark Twain! I never found anyone who was absolutely right – except, possibly, James MacTaggart, who wrote one [the episode 'Wish You Were Here'].

'We never got the right tone and I became frustrated with the series because it fell short. Even a lot of writers thought of it as *The Avengers*, but it wasn't. It was a real attempt to examine an era through the eyes of somebody to whom it would have been extraordinary, using wit throughout the storyline.'

Perhaps continual comparisons with *The Avengers* played a part in the early downfall of *Adam Adamant Lives!* but, fortunately for ABC, such comparisons had little effect on their long-running series, which ran for eight years (1961-9), and was later revisited as *The New Avengers*, although the sequel failed to attain the extraordinary levels of interest generated by its predecessor. One of the decade's most original shows, *The Avengers* oozed quality in its scripts, performances and direction. With its unique blend of style, wit, fantasy and drama, it was a production of the highest order. Who will ever forget the suave, bowler-hatted, umbrella-carrying John Steed (played by Patrick Macnee), and his sidekicks, most notably leather-clad beauties Cathy Gale (Honor Blackman) and Emma Peel (Diana Rigg)? Equally adept at not only fighting crime, thanks to their expertise in martial arts, but sending millions of male viewers' pulses into overdrive with their sexy looks and image, Gale and Peel were followed by Tara King (Linda Thorson), by which time the show was riding high in the States, too.

The programme was soon being transmitted in over a hundred countries, making it one of the most popular television series of all time, but its international appeal didn't begin in earnest until it started being made on film, thereby broadening its export potential. The Cathy Gale episodes weren't screened in the States until 1991, so for the majority of Americans their introduction to *The Avengers* was the Macnee-Rigg shows. This was a phase in the show's evolution which saw storylines adopt a more fantasy-based, surreal approach. The interplay between the two central characters was superb and for many people this is the show's most fondly remembered period.

The Avengers wouldn't have existed if an earlier series, *Police Surgeon*, starring Ian Hendry as Dr Geoffrey Brent, hadn't been cancelled unexpectedly after just twelve episodes. Producer Leonard White was told by Sydney Newman, then Head of Drama at ABC, to find a new vehicle for

OPPOSITE: Diana Rigg as Emma Peel was the first of Steed's companions seen by American audiences.

'They would go on and on until they got it right while the artists were exhausted.'

Hendry – and he only had nine weeks before it was due on air. Having to work at breakneck speed, it soon became a department problem to resolve. 'We decided to lose the obvious police element,' says White, 'and dreamed up an idea of avenging and beginning to be more undercover.' Hendry retained his doctor's status, but this time played David Keel instead of Geoffrey Brent, with the first season of *The Avengers* centring on Keel's attempts, with the help of John Steed (Macnee), to avenge the death of his fiancée, who unwittingly becomes caught up in a gunfight between rival gangs.

Steed was a supporting character during the first season and, if it hadn't been for an actors' strike, might have remained so. By the time the strike was resolved Hendry was unavailable after securing an attractive film contract, leaving White and the rest of the team in a dilemma. As a consequence of Hendry's departure, Steed was promoted from a support role to lead, but who was going to join him in the crusade to rid the world of crime? The predicament enabled White and his colleagues to introduce the new element of a woman in a leading role, as he explains: 'The whole ethos of women in television was that they occupied supporting roles – it was always the man in the lead. But things were changing.' Sydney Newman and Leonard White were admirers of Margaret Mead, the American anthropologist and photographer, and, inspired by Mead, they decided to present a female character in an entirely new way.

'I always wanted to see what it would be like actually putting a woman in the man's role in a series of this nature, so this was the perfect opportunity,' admits White. Along with two of his directors, Don Leaver and Peter Hammond, he had Honor Blackman at the top of his list to play Cathy Gale, although the initial three episodes after Hendry's departure saw Jon Rollason as Dr Martin King grab second billing. The next few episodes then saw Gale alternating with nightclub singer Venus Smith (played by Julie Stevens) until Venus was phased out after six episodes.

White recalls: 'I'd compiled a list of about five names for the part – all excellent actresses. I preferred Honor but took my list along to Sydney [Newman]. He reversed my list completely, putting Honor at the bottom and Nyree Dawn Porter at the top. Then he went off on holiday. I decided to go with Honor anyway and, fortunately, when he returned from holiday he didn't mind.'

Playing the liberated Cathy Gale was a happy time for Blackman, partly because she was treading new ground in the development of the female character in television.

'No woman had ever been permitted to be of equal intelligence and intellectual capacity to the man,' says Blackman. 'There had been two kinds of women: the loving, faithful one at home and the lady in black knickers, stockings and suspenders who lured the good man away. So to find a woman who was not only the equal in intelligence but quite a cool character who could physically defend herself was very exciting.'

An increasingly popular element of the shows was the fight sequences, for which Blackman was tutored in judo.

'In the second year, the fights became bigger and better and then they introduced two per show instead of one,' Blackman explains. 'The sequences were shot the night before the show with five cameras. It was great for the cameramen but absolute hell for the artists participating, especially when they said: "I didn't quite get that." They would go on and on until they got it right, while the artists were exhausted.'

Occasionally fights didn't go to plan, like the scene in a graveyard from the episode, 'Mandrake', where Blackman, who attended weekly judo lessons and reached the level of brown belt, accidentally split wrestler Jackie Pallo's nose, knocking him unconscious for over seven minutes.

'I was walking around this grave sobbing, "I'll never fight again." It was a nightmare. He was supposed to be wrestling that night in Dover but the doctor wouldn't let him go. I thought I'd ruined his career but the reverse was true because it was on the front of every paper.'

Honor Blackman stayed with the series two years before deciding to hang up her leathers for pastures new: before long, she was playing Pussy Galore in *Goldfinger*. Her character became popular with men and women.

'It was natural I'd get male fans,' she concedes, 'but I used to get lots of letters from women saying things like: "Good on you, you've led us in the right direction – what a role model." Women were thrilled. It was a chink in the armour of those who thought women were incapable of competing with men. A lot of men, though, were upset and I'd often get the "you think you're so bloody clever" attitude.'

On a couple of occasions, Blackman was even asked to step outside for a spot of fisticuffs! 'It was at parties, and fortunately I hadn't drunk enough to go. But I found that if a man wasn't confident himself, he could find a confident woman threatening.'

Blackman's departure led to the appointment of Diana Rigg as Emma Peel, although one-and-a-half episodes had Elizabeth Shepherd playing Peel in late 1964. All her scenes were subsequently re-shot when Rigg joined the cast. As the series moved to film and eventually colour, it was sold to the States and became a major success, often a crucial element in a programme's longevity. If a show failed to be picked up by an American channel, its chances of enjoying a prosperous life were slim, a fate which befell many home grown sci-fi and adventure shows.

Ask anyone to name America's most successful sci-fi programme and you can bet your bottom dollar they'll choose *Star Trek*. But despite the intrepid

ABOVE: Roberta Leigh's *Space Patrol* tackled their first missions in 1963.

Captain Kirk and his courageous and loyal crew, including the pointy-eared Spock, setting out in the *Starship Enterprise* on 'a five-year mission to boldly go where no man had gone before', the American station NBC lost interest after three years (eighty episodes) and gave them the chop.

First shown this side of the pond in 1969, Gene Roddenberry's show has become a money-spinning favourite around the world, spawning more merchandise than you could ever dream of: a series of big-screen blockbusters, a multitude of books and . . . well, the list is endless. I'm sure replicas of Spock's pointed ears were sold somewhere in the world, for he became the show's most memorable character. It is, therefore, surprising to learn that Roddenberry had a fight on his hands to retain the Vulcan. Not only did NBC executives worry that viewers wouldn't be able to relate to Spock, but Leonard Nimoy – who brought the character to life – wasn't sure about the pointed ears, fearing they would have a negative impact on his career. Roddenberry alleviated the actor's concerns by promising to drop the ears if he still wasn't convinced after the thirteenth episode. Nimoy was, of course, convinced and the rest is history.

There were threads of morality running through *Star Trek* storylines, including a multiracial crew showing that human beings can work together in peace and harmony regardless of colour or creed. Such beliefs were also to the fore in Roberta Leigh's puppet series, *Space Patrol*, which debuted in 1963 and subsequently became the most watched children's show in the States at that time, where it was known as *Planet Patrol* because of a home-grown series of the same name. Set in the year 2100, earthlings had formed the United Galactic Organization with beings from other planets, including Mars and Venus. Now regarded as a cult classic, viewers jumped on board *Galasphere 347* and rocketed around the solar system during the thirty-nine episodes. Such was its popularity that one fan, a respectable executive at a top advertising agency, turned the dashboard of his car into a replica of *Galasphere*'s flight deck.

Puppets were also the name of the game for Gerry Anderson, probably the most prolific producer in this field during the sixties. With his then wife, Sylvia, he created futuristic adventures of the highest quality, which, of course, didn't come cheaply. During the decade seven shows emerged from the Anderson stable, beginning with *Supercar*, which became a success on both sides of the Atlantic, a crucial factor considering the relatively high expenditure involved in making each series. In 1960, Gerry Anderson approached Granada with his plans for the shows, but after hearing nothing, a speculative phone call led to a meeting with Lew Grade, head of ATV, who commissioned the series for his international distribution branch, ITC.

Having the foresight to create the shows with more than just the British domestic market in mind paid dividends, not least in America, with printed scripts and the dialogue always Americanized. The stories' locations also had an American feel to them, beginning with *Supercar*'s Black Rock laboratory in the Nevada Desert. 'They were shows about sophisticated vehicles and machines, and at that time the only country capable of making items of that magnitude was America,' says Gerry Anderson. 'And, of course, unless you had the American market, you couldn't afford to spend a lot of money on the shows . . . and all my shows had one thing in common: they were all expensive at the time they were made.'

Surprisingly, Gerry Anderson

1960s ANDERSON PRODUCTIONS

1961-62 *Supercar* (39 episodes)

1962-63 *Fireball XL5* (39 episodes)

1964-65 *Stingray* (39 episodes)

1965-66 *Thunderbirds* (32 episodes)

1967-68 *Captain Scarlet and the Mysterons* (32 episodes)

1968-69 *Joe 90* (30 episodes)

1969 *The Secret Service* (13 episodes)

BELOW: Gerry and Sylvia Anderson prepare Mike Mercury's *Supercar* for another flight.

never intended to make a career out of animation. 'I certainly didn't want to go into animation, and the last thing in the world I wanted to do was work with puppets. The only reason I did was because having formed a production company [AP Films with Arthur Provis], we were unable to get any work.'

With funds running low, they were desperate for something to come along when Roberta Leigh asked them to make her puppet show, *The Adventures of Twizzle*. 'It's surprising what you'll do when you're on the breadline. I'd never seen a puppet in my life and grew to hate them very quickly.'

But Anderson seized the opportunity, believing that if he made a sterling job of the series, it would open up doors for making live-action pictures. What it did, however, was expose his talents in producing animation and led to an endless supply of work. Now, of course, he's happy with the success achieved, even if it wasn't planned.

Fireball XL5, which had a working title of *Century 21*, was transmitted by NBC in the States, a major coup, and soon after Lew Grade bought Anderson's production company. In 1964, Troy Tempest took the submarine

BELOW: *Thunderbird 2* is prepared for departure from her hangar on Tracey Island.

Stingray out on its inaugural mission. Anderson found it an exciting programme to produce, especially as he faced the challenge of filming underwater sequences. He says: 'We couldn't actually put the submarine in the water because it would have fallen apart, so shot it through an aquarium full of fish with *Stingray* positioned behind.'

Of all the shows Gerry Anderson has produced, most people would probably pick *Thunderbirds* and *Captain Scarlet and the Mysterons* as their favourites. '*Thunderbirds*, certainly,' agrees Anderson, who explains that with each episode's duration lengthened to fifty minutes, his team was able to dedicate more time to developing the characterizations. 'Then, if you put a character into jeopardy, the audience was more concerned because they knew the character better.'

Two of my own favourite characters from *Thunderbirds* were Brains and Parker.

'Brains with his pebble glasses and his stutter was a stereotype character at that time – it's how a lot of people saw scientists,' says Anderson. 'Parker was interesting because his voice was based on a waiter's who served at a pub in Cookham-on-Thames we'd visit for lunch. I sent David Graham, who supplied the voice of Parker, to the pub for lunch for a week so that he could listen to him.'

Between 1968 and 1969, a nine-year-old agent called *Joe 90* was entertaining millions of fans by embarking on espionage missions, while the Andersons saw out the decade with *The Secret Service*. The show's main character was Father Stanley Unwin, a vicar-cum-secret agent with BISHOP (British Intelligence Service Headquarters Operation Priest). Not only was the character named after the founder of the gibberish language, Unwinese, but Unwin provided the puppet's voice and appeared as Father Stanley in live-action sequences. Unlike Anderson's previous programmes, only thirteen instalments were made. After showing the pilot to Lew Grade, the chief of ATV didn't think the American audience would understand the use of Unwinese in the show. Believing it would alienate the audience, he decided to cancel the show after the first – and only – season.

ABOVE: Parker, a reformed villain, drove Lady Penelope's famous pink Rolls Royce.

'Parker was interesting because his voice was based on a waiter's who served at a pub in Cookham-on-Thames we'd visit for lunch.'

WHO'S WHO IN THE ANDERSON WORLD

Supercar's leading figure was heroic pilot Mike Mercury, who sat behind the controls of *Supercar*, a fabulous vehicle invented by Austrian and English scientists Professor Popkiss and Dr Beaker.

From an island base in the Pacific, the World Space Patrol had their own remarkable spaceship in *Fireball XL5*, with Colonel Steve Zodiac at the helm, ably assisted in his travels by Dr Venus (the ship's medical officer) and Professor Matic (navigator-cum-engineer), all reporting to Commander Zero.

Controlling the world's oceans was the responsibility of WASP (World Aquanaut Security Patrol), an unenviable task undertaken in a submarine called *Stingray*. In charge of the ship was the grey-suited, blue-eyed Captain Troy Tempest, a hero if ever you saw one; helping him in the submarine, which could travel at speeds of up to 600 knots, were Lieutenant Sheridan, as navigator and hydrophones operator, and Marina, a resident of the underwater city of Pacifica who offers her services – all legitimate, of course – in helping keep the waters trouble free.

Meanwhile, in the twenty-first century, the affluent Jeff Tracy dipped into his own pocket to fund a life-saving team called International Rescue, who piloted the *Thunderbirds*. Another organization operating from the Pacific, this time from their own, private Tracy Island, International Rescue involved all of Jeff's sons: Scott piloted *Thunderbird 1*, Virgil was in the hot seat of my favourite, the hefty green freighter known as *Thunderbird 2*, Alan was responsible for *Thunderbird 3*, Gordon was in control of the little yellow submarine, *Thunderbird 4*, and poor old John drew the short straw, spending most of his life floating around in the space station *Thunderbird 5*. Other memorable characters included Lady Penelope in her unforgettable pink Roller, driven by Aloysius 'Yes, m'lady' Parker, a one-time petty criminal. Then, of course, there was the aptly-named, bespectacled scientist, Brains.

By the year 2068, *Captain Scarlet* was on the scene. A crucial member of Spectrum, whose base was a flying aircraft carrier stationed high up in Earth's atmosphere, he reported to the hard-nosed war

ABOVE: Scott Tracey was always first at the scene of any disaster in *Thunderbird 1*.

OPPOSITE: Gerry and Sylvia Anderson pose in their office alongside Troy Tempest, looking high and dry without *Stingray*.

veteran, Colonel White. Other loyal servants of Spectrum included Captain Blue, Lieutenant Green, Captain Ochre, Captain Grey, Captain Magenta, Dr Fawn and the courageous flying Angels: Destiny, Symphony, Rhapsody, Melody and Harmony. Oh, and we shouldn't forget the baddie, Captain Black.

Back to 2013, and Joe from *Joe 90* – one of those know-all kids who would normally drive you mad, except he used his super-intelligence to good effect: preserving global peace, so how could you get annoyed with him? Nine-year-old Joe was adopted by Professor McClaine, whose claim to fame was creating the BIG RAT (Brain Impulse Galvanascope Record And Transfer), a strange, revolving machine that turned Joe, when he wore his special specs, into an all-round expert. Another character who was often around was McClaine's best friend, Sam Loover, who was deputy head of WIN (World Intelligence Network), for whom Joe was the leading agent.

The sixties closed with Anderson's *The Secret Service* introducing us to Father Stanley Unwin, who reported to The Bishop, who was in charge of Operation Priest at Whitehall. Assisting Unwin was blond-haired Matthew Harding, who was supposed to be twenty-eight but must have been fibbing because his careworn face made him look twenty years older. Harding was another full-time BISHOP agent, although he disguised himself as the vicarage gardener.

During the sixties, Lew Grade's prolific ITC stable produced a crop of well-received adventure series. *The Champions* spotlighted three superagents endowed with powers of telepathy who are employed by Geneva-based international crime-fighting agency, Nemesis. Playing superhuman agent Sharron Macready alongside William Gaunt and Stuart Damon, was Alexandra Bastedo, whose striking looks meant she quickly became a pin-up. She says: 'Everybody remembers me for *The Champions*. At the moment, I'm getting letters from the Czech Republic, Germany and America, so you can always tell where it's being shown. There were thirty hour-long episodes of the show, which took a year and three months to film. I've never worked so hard in my life. Often my day started at six in the morning. I was picked up and taken to the studio at seven-thirty, and was on the set by eight-thirty. We worked right through the week including every other Saturday. And when I finally got a day off, I ended up being dragged around various London boutiques looking for costumes my character could wear.'

When the first episode of *The Champions* was screened in 1968, the original promotional material issued the warning: 'Beware villains of the world, you've met your match', before explaining that the agents' mysterious superhuman powers, with which they were endowed following a plane crash in Tibet, would aid them in their 'fight against international crime and terrorism' – all gripping stuff.

The programme's popularity saw a twenty-year-old Bastedo catapulted into the spotlight, but she believes it happened too early in her career. 'After making a series like *The Champions* you can become typecast. Before the show began I'd had a more interesting career. Playing Sharron Macready cast me in a mould for considerable time before I eventually broke away and went on to play some wonderful parts. I don't regret the success of *The Champions*, I just wish it had happened later in my career – perhaps when I was about twenty-eight.'

Success brings the inevitable flood of fan mail – and not all the attention is welcome, as Bastedo explains: 'One situation got quite serious. This woman, who was a lesbian, had left her husband and brought her two kids to my house with the intention of living with me in England! In the end, I had to call the police. My flatmate, who was an air hostess, wanted to get off to work but couldn't because we had this woman

'I'm getting letters from the Czech Republic, Germany and America, so you can always tell where it's being shown.'

outside the door shouting, "God will punish you!" The police ended up calling a priest to try to persuade her to go home.'

Another offering from ITC was a story about a ghost in a white suit – remember *Randall and Hopkirk (Deceased)*? Chances are you do, perhaps because of the 2000 remake starring Vic Reeves and Bob Mortimer. One of ITC's most successful series, twenty-six ghostly tales were shown between 1969 and 1970 – not bad when you consider that one half of the duo is killed off in the first episode. It was a rather unique premise: Marty Hopkirk (brought to life by Kenneth Cope, most recently seen as Ray Hilton in *Brookside*) and Jeff Randall (played by the late Mike Pratt) were private investigators, whose friendship and working relationship were shattered when Marty was killed by a hit-and-run driver. Later, his spirit – only visible to Jeff – appeared wearing a startling white suit to help his partner hunt the man who sent him to an early grave. This marked the first of many cases the duo solved together.

Being offered the chance to play a character who dies in the opening episode of a new series doesn't sound overly promising for one's career but, fortunately for Kenneth Cope, he didn't let that put him off accepting the role of Marty. Spotted in a Soho restaurant by director Cyril Frankel, Cope was called to the studio for an audition, the first step in what was to become fourteen months of intense work. But he'll never forget that initial meeting. 'I was told: "We want you to star in a series, but you get

BELOW: Stuart Damon and William Gaunt were the other two Nemesis super-agents in *The Champions*.

'We want you to star in a series, but you get killed in the first episode.'

killed in the first episode." There was a long pause before the casting director added: "But you come back as a ghost."'

Once his screen character was killed, Cope donned a white suit – or rather, suits, because he had five bought from Savile Row – for the remaining episodes. The suits became a trademark but were obviously prone to getting dirty. 'They were constantly being pressed and dry-cleaned, and if we noticed any marks during filming, it would be covered up with this white stuff, like Tipp-Ex. The suits could stand up on their own by the end of the show,' jokes Cope, who believes visiting actors must have thought he was 'potty' at times.

'To save the suits getting creased or marked, I'd take them off at the end of shooting. So there I was, standing in white boots, yellow underpants, white shirt and tie – I must have looked a sight.'

And he probably did, especially if he was wearing his wig back-to-front. 'Everyone had bushy hair in those days but as I was losing mine, we thought a wig was the answer. Unfortunately, the hairdresser put it on the wrong way round for the first two episodes – no one really knew, though.'

BELOW: Kenneth Cope with Mike Pratt and Annette André as Jeanie in *Randall and Hopkirk (Deceased)*.

Although Cope admits that being out of circulation for fourteen months making *Randall and Hopkirk (Deceased)* was followed by two years' unemployment, he's immensely proud of playing the ghost. 'What I liked was that the whole family could watch the programme. Mums and dads were never embarrassed by it because there were no sexual scenes – and the kids loved it, too.'

Much earlier in ITC's life, back in 1962 to be precise, a man with a trademark halo above a perfectly groomed, slicked hairdo went about his taxing duties with an incessant smile on his face. Without ever putting a hair out of place, and always emerging triumphant from a myriad of close shaves and scrapes, *The Saint* was a man you could have faith in and rely upon to weed out the baddies with aplomb.

Using, at first, storylines based on Leslie Charteris's novels, the indefatigable team of Monty Berman and Robert S. Baker created one of the British television industry's longest-running adventure series; for seven years (1962 to 1969) it ran on home soil, but its success stretched far beyond Blighty, aided by the numerous international settings adopted in the stories, even if most scenes were shot in a British studio.

Upon acquiring the rights to adapt Charteris's novels for the small screen, Baker and Berman quickly secured a commission from Lew Grade's ATV, even though Associated Rediffusion had been offered the project first. Such was Grade's confidence in the show's potential that he commissioned a season of twenty-six episodes to be made on film to increase the likelihood of selling the product abroad – a decision he never regretted because it struck gold all over the world, selling to over sixty countries.

Playing smoothie Simon Templar was Roger Moore, who was in Italy when his agent called to say Lew Grade wanted to meet to discuss a new show.

'In 1957, whilst making the Ivanhoe series, I was afraid that I wouldn't make another film for the cinema,' admits Moore. 'There was a stigma attached to television actors returning to the big screen, and so I thought that *The Saint* might be a good vehicle for me to obtain the rights to, and make a television series. At that time, Leslie Charteris wasn't interested in the proposition and as luck had it, before I could pursue any other avenues I received a call to return to Hollywood to make *The Miracle* for Warner Brothers. A few years and a few films later, I was in Italy making a couple of pictures when I received a call from my agent saying that Lew Grade wanted to meet me about a television series called *The Saint*, which he was putting together.'

Moore had read many of Charteris's novels and was convinced they could be adapted successfully for the small screen. As for creating his screen character, he says: 'To be honest, whatever happens on the first day of shooting is what the audience is stuck with in what might follow. I just played it as I felt I should and could. As always, I just played myself.'

As well as the halo and the impeccable dress sense, one of *The Saint*'s trademarks was the sleek white Volvo he drove. But if events had unfolded as planned, Moore says the character would have driven a Jag. 'We originally wanted to purchase a Jaguar, but were told by Jaguar that they couldn't deliver a car to us in under three months. We needed a vehicle straight away. Johnny Goodman, the production manager, showed me a still of the P1800, and I thought it looked terrific.

'We bought two straight away and they were both on the road in three days. I bought one of them and used it to drive to and from the studio. It was my favourite car and I remain very, very fond of it. In fact, I drive a Volvo today.'

Within months of transmitting in Britain, the show was topping the ratings and remained a favourite among the viewing public for the rest of its screen life. For the last forty-seven episodes of the series, Roger Moore stepped up to become co-producer with Baker, forming the Bamore

BELOW: The Volvo driven by Roger Moore in *The Saint* was originally intended to have been a Jaguar, but Jaguar could not deliver a vehicle in time for filming.

production company in the process, while Monty Berman headed off to produce other adventure series, including *The Baron* and, of course, the aforementioned *The Champions, Department S* and *Randall and Hopkirk (Deceased)*.

The Baron (1966-1967), a much underrated series, continued the fashion for importing American actors to play tough, no-nonsense leads, with Steve Forrest cast as antiques-expert-cum-agent, John Mannering. Based on a character created by author John Creasey, Mannering was hired to solve crimes around the world, just like the formidable trio from *Department S*, a further adventure series from ATV's international arm, ITC. Again produced by Berman, *Department S* was the name given to a special section of Interpol. Another American actor, this time Joel Fabiani, was cast as one of the leads, playing Stewart Sullivan, working alongside Jason King (Peter Wyngarde, who went on to star in his own series in the seventies) and Annabelle Hurst (Rosemary Nicols). While Sullivan and Hurst conducted their enquiries in a fairly conventional manner, the sunny, flamboyant, author-cum-agent King was distinctly unconventional in the way he executed his duties. But, like all agents from this era, they relentlessly solved their crimes with relative ease, even if they had to endure the odd scratch along the way.

For many, the jewel in the crown of ITC's array of adventure-espionage series is one of the most underrated: *Man in a Suitcase*. Thirty hour-long episodes were shown between 1967 and 1968 with another American, silver-haired Richard Bradford, playing the lead role as McGill. The character was a tough, sceptical former US intelligence agent who was booted out of his job after being incorrectly accused of wrongdoing. Exiled to England, he became a freelance troubleshooter and private eye to earn a crust. If the price was right, McGill was your man and he was hired for all manner of jobs.

One of ITC's most realistic shows, created by Richard Harris and Dennis Spooner, there was an earthiness about the production and scripts. McGill was not the kind of debonair, genteel adventurer who hardly put a hair out of place during troubled moments; instead, he really got his hands dirty in order to solve a case, and often found himself on the receiving end of some brutally harsh treatment. These elements made the series stand out from other ITC shows and made it incredibly popular with its fans.

Richard Bradford, who now lives in California, believes he was offered the job on the back of his performance in *The Chase*, a film with Marlon Brando.

'I guess Lew Grade saw the movie and was interested,' says Bradford. I'd done a couple of things on TV, one movie and a little bit on Broadway, but that was about it. I hadn't travelled out of the country so here was the chance to go to England and play a character I loved and felt good about.'

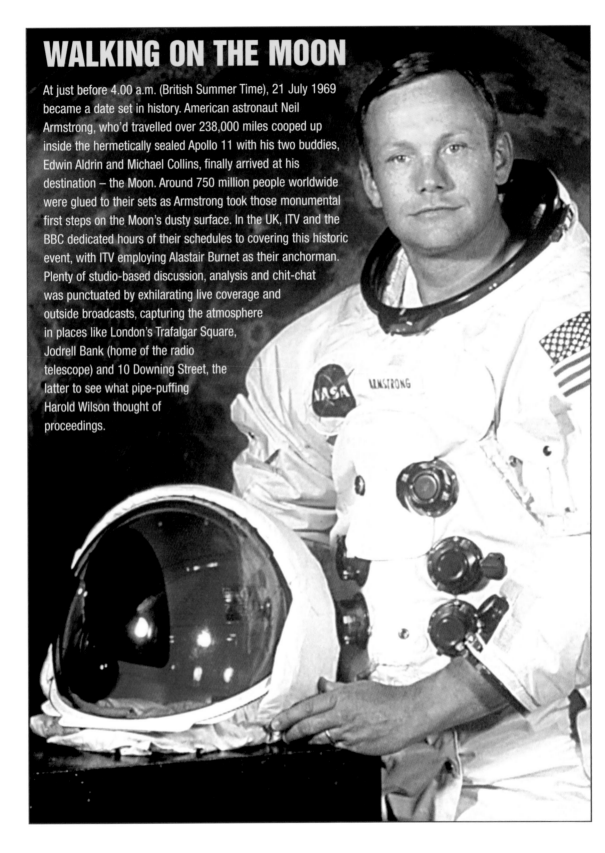

WALKING ON THE MOON

At just before 4.00 a.m. (British Summer Time), 21 July 1969 became a date set in history. American astronaut Neil Armstrong, who'd travelled over 238,000 miles cooped up inside the hermetically sealed Apollo 11 with his two buddies, Edwin Aldrin and Michael Collins, finally arrived at his destination – the Moon. Around 750 million people worldwide were glued to their sets as Armstrong took those monumental first steps on the Moon's dusty surface. In the UK, ITV and the BBC dedicated hours of their schedules to covering this historic event, with ITV employing Alastair Burnet as their anchorman. Plenty of studio-based discussion, analysis and chit-chat was punctuated by exhilarating live coverage and outside broadcasts, capturing the atmosphere in places like London's Trafalgar Square, Jodrell Bank (home of the radio telescope) and 10 Downing Street, the latter to see what pipe-puffing Harold Wilson thought of proceedings.

Sadly, the series didn't take off in the States, partly, Bradford admits, because of the stiff competition. 'It wasn't well known because it was shown Friday nights up against *Star Trek*, and viewers were reluctant to switch. I still hear, though, from people who saw it and they still remember it – I don't know why. I know we were successful to a certain degree, but it wasn't what it could have been. It hurts me that it wasn't as good as it should have been. I'm sure a lot of it's my fault, but other people are to blame also.'

What other shows were stretching our imaginations, exploiting the indefinable boundaries between fact and fiction in the medium of space? Shortlived it may have been, but *A for Andromeda*, transmitted in 1961, and the sequel, *The Andromeda Breakthrough*, shown a year later, marked a significant step in the BBC's development of science fiction for adults. The esteemed astronomer, writer and Cambridge University professor, Sir Frederick Hoyle, developed a storyline which was adapted for the small screen by BBC producer John Elliot. Here was a sci-fi series that appeared to have some basis in science fact rather than in a world of pure fantasy. Professor Hoyle believed that the most likely method of making contact with alien worlds was by listening for signals with a radio telescope.

Set high in the Yorkshire Dales in 1970, *A for Andromeda* opened with scientists completing the final checks on just such a new radio-telescope. When a message originating millions of light years away within the constellation of Andromeda is intercepted, eager young scientist, John Fleming, played by Peter Halliday, records the signal and unravels the curious sequence of dots and dashes.

He discovers that the message gives instructions on how to build a computer, the likes of which has never been seen before. The government steps in and decide to construct the computer at an isolated rocket establishment on the Western Isles but, as the *Radio Times* reported prior to the second episode being screened, 'Project Andromeda is classified Top Secret . . . but it is a secret for which certain people are prepared to kill.' The series was described as showing 'the impact of an alien intelligence upon life on Earth, and of the ruthless pursuit by rival factions of a secret on which the future of mankind may depend.' The BBC were certainly beefing up their new series, which began life when Hoyle originally dictated it on to a tape recorder for John Elliot to dramatize. As well as Halliday, the cast included Esmond Knight, Mary Morris and Julie Christie.

Peter Halliday holds happy memories of making the series. 'We went down to South Wales and stayed at Tenby, then filmed in an old army camp on the cliffs near Manorbier. It was wonderful and we had a lot of fun, though we worked very hard, too, scrambling around on cliffs and splashing into the sea.'

Halliday enjoyed working with the rest of the team but was saddened to hear Julie Christie wouldn't be free to reprise her role in the sequel. Christie, not long out of drama school, played both lab assistant, Christine, and Andromeda. When the computer the scientists built provided instructions on how to create a living organism, Christine seemed almost forced into committing suicide, leaving the organism the chance to grow and take on the identity of the pretty lab assistant. After the success of *A for Andromeda*, Christie found herself in demand and before long had launched her film career. When a movie contract prevented her appearance in *The Andromeda Breakthrough*, Susan Hampshire took over. Halliday, though, didn't regard the sequel as so successful. 'It was a rather diffused story and I don't think it did particularly well, whereas *A for Andromeda* had a rattling good story, which moved like a bullet.'

Casting for the original series was the responsibility of director Michael Hayes, who spotted Julie Christie at the Central School of Speech and Drama in London, playing Anne Frank in a student matinee. So successful was Christie in her role in *A for Andromeda* that when the idea for a sequel was mooted, Hayes recommended that his colleagues sign up the actress pronto. 'At the end of the recordings for the first series, there was a small party and I was walking across the bridge at Television Centre with Julie and Donald Baverstock, who was programme controller at the time. I said to him: "If they're going to do a sequel, sign this girl up now because you'll lose her if you don't." They decided not to sign her up and, of course, lost her. They got Susan Hampshire, but I don't think it was the same.'

Counterstrike (1969), another sci-fi offering, didn't exactly set the world alight in terms of audience figures, with only the closing episode, 'The Mutant', charting in the Top 20 of most-watched programmes that year. Many national papers reported its demise in November 1969, and appeared genuinely saddened about Simon King (played by Jon Finch) being prematurely kicked into space. Although low budgets meant special effects weren't high on the agenda, *Counterstrike*'s regular audience was keen to follow the adventures of King, an agent from the Intergalactic Congress sent to Earth to help prevent aliens from the far-off Centauran star system taking over.

In a document written prior to the launch of the show, producer Patrick Alexander outlined the scenario: 'The stars that warm one of the planets of the constellation Centaurus are dying out; so its inhabitants – who represent a civilization more advanced than ours – are looking for somewhere else to go. They have invaded our Earth, a more backward planet, to wipe out the population and take over. As a counter-move to this, the Intergalactic Congress (a "United Nations" representing worlds rather than nations) has sent a representative, Martin Cain [later changed to Simon Cain and, finally, Simon King], to help ward off the threat and to defeat the efforts of two Centaurans who have already consolidated a business operation in England as a front. Both Cain and the Centaurans look and behave overtly just like the other "human beings" of our planet.'

As Alexander pointed out, the series was based more on 'science fact rather than science fantasy'. But when the programme finally made it to our screens, its life was short. Mystified by the show's abandonment, the *Daily Sketch* remarked: 'Those wicked aliens, scheming to own the world, couldn't do it – kill off Jon Finch, hero of the BBC1's sci-fi series, *Counterstrike*. But the BBC had no such problem. With a blue pencil instead of an atomic blaster, they have doomed the show and taken both Mr Finch and the series out of orbit, firmly off the screen. There are no plans to make any more. It all seems rather odd.'

The reporter noted that the show was, apparently, axed to make way for *Take Three Girls*, stating: 'But *Girls* on its present showing may not be as big a draw.'

AROUND THE WORLD   1967

The year opened just as the previous one had finished, with a tragic death: Donald Campbell was killed in his boat, *Bluebird*, while attempting to break the world water-speed record on Coniston Water, in the Lake District. Two months later, in March, the Cornish coastline and its marine life were under threat when the 61,000-ton oil tanker, *Torrey Canyon*, foundered in waters between the Scilly Isles and Land's End. The bill to legalize abortion was on course to become law before the end of the year, while on the transport front, the £29 million *QE2* was launched from Clydebank in September, and the world's first supersonic aircraft, the Anglo-French Concorde, made its debut appearance in Toulouse (below). The year also saw the emergence of flower power and hippies, cash machines and breathalysers in Britain. Colour TV was finally launched in the UK, thanks to BBC2, although sets were initially prohibitively expensive and unreliable: it wasn't until the mid-seventies that most people finally ditched their black-and-white sets.

ROBERTA LEIGH

Space Patrol wasn't Roberta Leigh's only association with interplanetary travel. Leigh's earlier children's series, *Torchy the Battery Boy* (right), about a toy with a magical bulb on his hat which helped him find lost objects, saw her character head off into space. When some children attach their toys to kites while playing in Mr Bumble-Drop's garden, and they're blown away by a strong gust of wind, Torchy comes to the rescue and discovers they're marooned on a faraway star, resulting in a dangerous mission in a cardboard rocket to rescue the toys.

As well as *Sara and Hoppity* (see page 31) and the earlier *Adventures of Twizzle*, Leigh's other work in the medium includes the lesser-known *Paul Starr*, for which a pilot episode filmed in colour followed the men of the Space Bureau of Investigation. Sadly, no series materialized. Continuing the space theme, *The Solarnauts* was a venture into live-action for Leigh, although, again, only a pilot was made. Three further children's shows included *Picture the Word*, shown as part of ITV's *Small Time* season; *Wonderboy and Tiger*, concerning a boy who flew on his magic carpet with Tiger, his magic cat, whose whiskers would sparkle when someone needed their help; and *Send for Dithers*, a series of thirteen episodes about a dithery man who ran a breakdown service. Every time he was called to help he'd end up causing more problems. Then, there was *The Adventures of Mr Hero!*, based on books written by Leigh. Unfortunately this was deemed too expensive to make by the television company that had expressed an interest and all that exists is a 1966 pilot.

The idea for *Counterstrike* was first discussed in 1966, three years before it eventually made it onto the screen. A pilot, 'Mark of Cain', was made, but in January 1967 further development was brought to a halt when the BBC decided to hold it 'in reserve as a replacement programme', perhaps because the idea was too similar to *The Invaders*, which was being aired on ITV during that period. But by the summer, Paul Fox, then controller of BBC1, had watched the pilot, liked what he saw, and wanted to turn it into a thirteen-part series for screening between July and September 1968. In the end only ten episodes of *Counterstrike* were made, with the broadcasts commencing in September 1969, but only nine of the ten actually saw the light of day, one being shelved to make way for a documentary about the Kray court case.

Of course, no book about television in the sixties would be complete without mention of *The Prisoner*, such was its impact when the seventeen episodes were screened between 1967 and 1968. Imaginative, intriguing and allegorical, it's a series that has baffled and engrossed viewers in equal measures for almost forty years. Repeated on Channel 4 during the eighties, the series has become a cult classic that every TV aficionado simply has to have in their DVD library.

At the heart of *The Prisoner* was Patrick McGoohan's superb performance as Number Six, a British secret agent who quits his job only to be abducted and spirited away to a mysterious village, where the sun always shines on the equally mysterious, bizarrely dressed residents. However, as Number Six quickly comes to realize, none of his fellow 'guests' – whether they are former agents like Number Six, serving agents spying on him, or medical staff in a village that seems to be part rest-and-recuperation centre and part prison – is quite as desperate to escape as he is. It transpires that, believing Number Six planned to defect to the other side of the Iron Curtain, his own superiors have whisked him off to this futuristic village to discover what information he may or may not have passed to the enemy. Any attempts he makes to break out are thwarted by an oversized bouncing balloon that engulfs and smothers fugitives.

The big boss, Number One, was never seen, while Number Two changed frequently, partly because failure wasn't tolerated and they all

ABOVE: Patrick McGoohan as *The Prisoner* and, below, with the dreaded big, white ball.

found Number Six too hard a nut to crack. Unlike the others who ended up in the village, Number Six was strong-willed, resolute and able to resist whatever pressure his tormentors brought to bear.

Abstract, psychedelic and, in sixties' parlance, 'far out', *The Prisoner* was made by Patrick McGoohan and Dave Tomblin's Everyman Films, with the finance provided by ITC. The series asked so many questions, with the questions as well as the answers open to your own interpretation, that you needed to take a complete rest after watching an episode until your head stopped spinning. It was fascinating stuff and it's not surprising that the programme, devised by McGoohan, still has legions of devoted fans around the world. Always enjoyable as an adventure yarn, *The Prisoner* also worked on many other levels and digging deeper revealed a myriad of ideas being explored through the programme. Number Six's refusal to accept the anonymous number that replaced his own name, declaring: 'I am not a number, I am a free man!', is also a refusal to be sucked into conformity, a rejection of authority and a demand to be allowed to exercise the right to remain an individual with a voice. The themes of protest and rebellion fitted the mood of the sixties and made *The Prisoner* the most fascinating of all adventure series from that decade.

The series was filmed partly on location in the pretty village of Portmeirion, which was designed by architect Clough Williams-Ellis and built on his own private peninsula on the North Wales coast. If it seemed familiar to some viewers, that's probably because it had featured in episodes of McGoohan's earlier espionage series, *Danger Man*, in which he played John Drake, a troubleshooter for NATO's secret service department. A slick production coupled with high-quality scripts and McGoohan's inimitable performances meant only one outcome – success. Thirty-nine half-hour episodes were transmitted between 1960 and 1961, with a further forty-five instalments, extended to an hour and screened in America as *Secret Agent*, arriving between 1964 and 1967. By the time McGoohan stepped into Number Six's shoes (we never did find out his real name) in *The Prisoner*, he was an instantly recognizable face.

While virtually everyone remembers *The Prisoner*, the same can't be said about *Dimensions of Fear*, a brief serial from ABC aired in January 1963 and starring, among others, Katharine Blake as Dr Barbara Finch, and Peter Copley as Professor Meredith. Based on a story by Berkely Mather, John Lucarotti supplied the scripts, which told the story of a research establishment in a sleepy English village. Scientists there studied how best to feed astronauts in space, but the unexplained deaths of two men soon caused fear among local residents. Perhaps the most obvious reason why *Dimensions of Fear* failed to capture the imagination of the viewing public in the same way that *The Prisoner* did is because there were only ever four forty-five-minute episodes.

OPPOSITE: Along with highlights from the Wimbledon tennis tournament, the western series *The Virginian* was one of the first programmes to be broadcast in colour in the UK.

THE INTRODUCTION OF COLOUR TV

Broadcasting in colour was being discussed as far back as 1943, but for various reasons, not least the technological limitations, another two decades were to pass before it finally became a reality. During the years when colour television remained a distant dream, those who couldn't wait to find out the colour of their favourite actress's dress could buy a colourizing filter which, after being placed over the black-and-white screen, turned the pictures into somewhat garish examples of colour – it was all rather primitive.

In America, CBS began 'Field Tests' of their colour system in 1941, broadcasting only to CBS staff as colour TV sets were not yet available to the public. As in Britain, however, the Second World War interfered, with technological developments for civilian use shelved in favour of the war efforts.

Different colour broadcasting systems vied for supremacy in the States in the early fifties, but the first coast-to-coast colour broadcast was made by NBC when they covered the Californian Tournament of the Roses on 1 January 1954.

Boffins at the Beeb experimented throughout the fifties but, unlike in America, there was neither the commercial pressure to be first into the market with a colour system nor an affluent viewing public with enough disposable income to be relied upon to go out and buy a new TV set capable of receiving colour transmissions. By the early sixties, when there were 12 million TV sets in the UK, compared with only 1 million in the early fifties, it was clear that the public were enthusiastic enough about TV for the next major step in broadcasting to be taken. But it wasn't until BBC2 officially launched its limited colour transmission on 1 July 1967 that this major advancement in the medium finally

arrived. Shows selected to receive the colour treatment included that year's Wimbledon coverage, but the progression of colour TV was hampered by the fact that colour TV sets were cumbersome, costly, unreliable and, it seems, dangerous. A series of house fires led to viewers being advised to keep an eye on their set for an hour after switching it off.

By 1968, some ITV companies were getting in on the act, and in May 1969 the Postmaster General gave the green light for BBC1 and ITV to begin their colour services, but unfolding the new spectacle to the entire UK was agonizingly slow. By 1972 only 17 per cent of households had colour television receivers. Improving technology resulted in smaller, cheaper and more reliable sets, and by the mid-seventies the relentless march of colour television had well and truly begun.

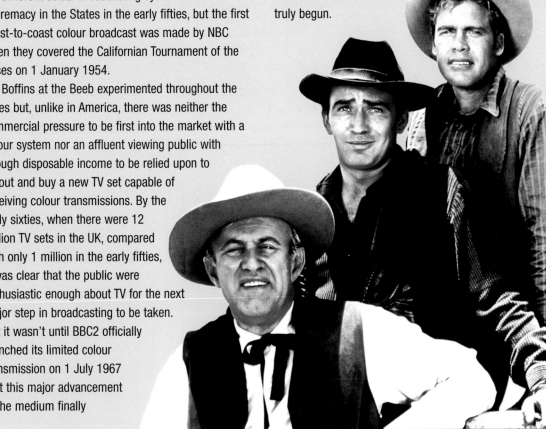

DRAMA

In the world of television drama, programme makers have the opportunity to focus on every conceivable aspect of society, yet, more often than not, when a scriptwriter begins formulating the outline for a new drama series, doctors, policemen and private investigators are the most popular professions to adopt for one's leading character. The sixties was no different in this respect and a plethora of cop shows, medical dramas and detective series were crammed into the schedules. But there was a shift in emphasis, particularly within the genre of police series, from the previous decade.

OPPOSITE: Nyree Dawn Porter in the 1967 costume drama *The Forsyte Saga*.

BELOW: Stratford Johns heads the cast in the police series *Softly, Softly*.

Of course, heavy overcoats, trilby hats and careering around the streets in black Morris Oxfords or Wolseleys were still in vogue, but the conservatism and placidity of shows such as *Dixon of Dock Green*, which ran from 1955 to 1976, were gradually replaced by a new wave of programmes depicting the realism of street life during the period. There was still room on our screens for the gentler approach to policing, like the tea-and-scones image of *Parkin's Patch* (see page 171), where the rural bobby rarely dealt with anything more serious than sheep rustling. In general, however, vapid, slow-moving productions were being superseded by faster-paced, grittier programmes that packed a punch, of which there is no finer example than *Z Cars*.

Following hot on the heels of a four-part drama, *Jacks and Knaves*, which focused on cases handled by Liverpudlian policemen, Troy Kennedy Martin's *Z Cars* was set in the same part of the world. Viewers first heard its distinctive theme music, based on the old Liverpudlian folksong, 'Johnny Todd', on 2 January 1962. It was during the previous year, while lying in bed with mumps, that Kennedy Martin originated the idea for *Z Cars*, for which he also suggested an alternative title – *Crime Car*.

'I was listening to police radio messages and was amazed at how young the policemen were,' recalls Kennedy Martin. 'It gave me the idea of doing something about young policemen, who were a bit out of their depth, dealing with people who were as old as their dad – perhaps involved in domestic quarrels and such like.'

Unlike *Dixon of Dock Green*, where investigations ran smoothly and crimes were always solved, *Z Cars* took a more realistic approach. Kennedy Martin says: 'There could be confusion at times and the young coppers wouldn't always get everything right.'

Originally, Kennedy Martin – who has since written many screenplays, including that of the original, classic movie *The Italian Job* – intended setting the series in London, mainly because he 'automatically assumed' it would be a requirement. Elwyn Jones, then head of the Documentary Drama Department within BBC Drama, had other ideas, as Kennedy Martin explains: 'He said: "Why don't you set it in the north?" He'd just done a little series, which, thankfully, I hadn't seen because it would have put me off my stroke, and it had been set in Liverpool with the Lancashire Police.'

Happy with Jones's suggestion, Kennedy Martin headed north and conducted some research with the constabulary. 'My eyes were opened by the way the beat operated.'

Kennedy Martin was employed by the Beeb as a script editor, and *Z Cars* marked his arrival on the writing scene, causing a stir when initially transmitted. Although popular with viewers from day one, the programme was deemed controversial by some, particularly the police. 'Members of

OPPOSITE: Jack Warner shows off his sergeant's stripes as *Dixon of Dock Green* in 1964.

the Police Union came down to London on the overnight train, arriving at the Director General's office at 10.00 a.m., complaining about the script,' says Kennedy Martin. 'The Chief of Police [Lancashire Constabulary] wasn't happy about the disorderly behaviour of the policemen in the series. One of them had punched his wife, giving her a black eye.'

Contrasting views were expressed from the Detective Superintendent downwards. 'They'd say: "Show us how we really are, give us the real thing. Don't say that we clean up every time because we don't."'

In reality, everyone knows that many crimes remain unsolved, and *Z Cars* provided an intriguing alternative to the solve-all-crimes premise of other police series. Yet some people were uncomfortable when such realities received exposure in a television drama. Kennedy Martin recalls a change of attitude at the BBC: 'The BBC said they weren't going to alter their stance on it, but they did. They gave this strong commitment that nothing was going to change, but much more control started coming down on the scripts, although from the beginning there had been pressure from the producer, who went through the script and objected to anything about policemen

BELOW: Frank Windsor, James Ellis, Stratford Johns, Joe Brady, Colin Welland, Robert Keegan and Donald Gee of *Z Cars*.

nipping off work to make bets, and all that stuff.'

Reflecting on the police's reaction to the start of the series, W. A. Roberts, former Detective Chief Superintendent and head of the Lancashire CID, wrote in the *Radio Times* on 16 December 1965: 'The elders of the Police Service were, to put it mildly, rather shocked, because . . . the programme showed policemen surreptitiously smoking on duty and having a quiet flutter on the horses. This was not the way, the elders said, in which the image of the police should be projected to the public.'

Set north of Liverpool in the fictitious Newtown, just one of the many overspill towns springing up all over the country, Kennedy Martin and Allan Prior wrote the early scripts. When Kennedy Martin moved on to pastures new, the workload was shared between a team of writers who scripted the stories concerning the day-to-day work of the crime patrol cars. As Kennedy Martin detailed in his original treatment: 'The series should be hard, tough, and realistic, with an abundance of northern humour.' He added: 'A series of this nature should eschew the magazine-type image which even affects *Coronation Street* and *Emergency – Ward 10*. The series should aim at a new, tougher and exciting pattern of entertainment which realistically reflects the life of this part of the nation, a pattern of entertainment which is already paying dividends in our contemporary film, theatre and novel.'

Becoming twice-weekly in 1967, over 600 episodes were broadcast during the show's lifetime, making many of its stars household names and spawning several spin-offs, including *Softly, Softly* (1966-9), which matured into *Softly, Softly: Task Force* (1969-76) and *Barlow at Large* (1971-3), which developed into *Barlow* (1971-3). Later on in *Z Cars'* run, genuine casebook material was provided, partly by two former high-ranking policemen who were assigned as advisers to the programme. As Elwyn Jones, writing in the *Radio Times* on the eve of the show's hundredth episode, stated: 'It is a programme about the police. It is not about crime; it is not about criminals; it is about those men without whom we could not sleep easily in our beds.'

While *Z Cars* featured bobbies on the beat, ATV's *Ghost Squad* – which ran in its original format between 1961 and 1963 before returning, a year later, under a new title, *G.S.5* – centred on the activities of Scotland Yard's International Investigation Division. The inspiration behind the series, written by a string of scriptwriters, was a novel by Detective Superintendent John Gosling. On screen, Sir Donald Wolfit was pulling the strings as Sir Andrew Wilson, while Angela Browne was cast as Helen Winters and Michael Quinn as agent Nick Craig.

> 'Show us how we really are, give us the real thing. Don't say that we clean up every time because we don't.'

AROUND THE WORLD 1968

April saw the tragic death of civil rights campaigner Dr Martin Luther King (right) when he was assassinated in Memphis. In May, a forty-five-year-old London man became the UK's first heart transplant patient. Student protests in France erupted into violence with rioting in the streets of Paris, while workers striking in support of the students brought France to a standstill. In June, Senator Robert Kennedy, younger brother of the assassinated President John F. Kennedy, was himself killed by a gunman. In the same month the comedy world mourned the loss of actor Tony Hancock, who committed suicide in Australia. However, there was more uplifting news in December when Apollo 8 orbited the moon.

Another arm of the police service became the focus of *Fraud Squad*. Again from ATV, there were twenty-six hour-long episodes entertaining viewers between 1969 and 1970. The show followed the crime-busting partnership of Detective Inspector Gamble and Detective Sergeant Vicky Hicks, played by Patrick O'Connell and Joanna Van Gyseghem. Tackling fraud of all shapes and sizes, *Fraud Squad* was the brainchild of Ivor Jay, who had worked as a scriptwriter on, among others, *Dixon of Dock Green* and *Crossroads*. His show, based on the work of a real fraud squad in Birmingham, was one of the first police series to feature an actress in a starring role.

Jay's daughter, Sue Jay, says that during her father's career as a journalist, he came to know the local superintendent, Jack Lashley, who became a key influence when considering storylines: 'My father thought the human stories behind the cases, which on the surface may have sounded dull, were a rich source of drama. One day he was talking to Lew

Grade at a party and told him of his idea. Lew shouted to one of the ATV executives: "Ivor's got just the thing we're looking for." And there it was – commissioned. *Fraud Squad* was hugely successful, sometimes beating *Coronation Street* in the ratings, and only came to an end when the lead actor decided to leave and live abroad.'

Ivor Jay was the originator and writer of another top-rated series from the sixties, *Deadline Midnight*. Aired between 1960 and 1961, the series was set in Fleet Street at the fictional offices of the *Daily Globe*, with Peter Vaughan and subsequently Glyn Houston in the editor's chair.

Sue Jay explains that, just like *Fraud Squad*, the idea stemmed from her father's days as a reporter. 'He'd always been interested in drama and writing, and when he was in Iraq during the Second World War, he wrote his first play for the troops. After the war he got a job with his local paper, the *Walsall Observer*. He then moved to Birmingham and the *Evening Dispatch* where he became a leader writer and film critic. When the *Dispatch* merged with the *Evening Mail* he was asked to tackle the relatively new medium of television and become a TV critic.

'He got to know many of the stars of the time. One of the friends he made was Lew Grade, whose company, ATV, was based in Birmingham. My father was keen to get into this new and exciting medium of television and came up with an idea for a drama series set in a daily newspaper. He thought the vast number of stories and the range of characters offered by the production of a newspaper with its relentless daily deadline offered drama, tension, humour and infinite variety. He called it *Deadline Midnight*. Lew Grade liked the idea and commissioned it immediately.'

The oil business is another source of high drama for television. The oil-related images that immediately spring to mind are, of course, the overgrown stetsons, Southfork Ranch and the Ewings of *Dallas* from the eighties. But the Beeb was wallowing in oil long before then, thanks to a show entitled *Mogul*, later relaunched as *The Troubleshooters*. Thirteen episodes of the former were transmitted in 1965, but with its new identity introduced for the second series a year later, the programme makers struck a gusher and the programme took off, stretching to over one hundred episodes and running through until 1972.

BELOW: Head of ATV, Lew Grade, commissioned the Ivor Jay series *Fraud Squad* and *Deadline Midnight* on the spur of the moment.

The idea to follow the activities of Mogul International, whose business was spread around the globe, came from writer John Elliot. In the beginning, though, Elliot experienced problems getting the project off the ground, despite initial interest from the Beeb. While dining at the Surrey home of Peter Graham Scott, who became the show's first producer, Elliot explained his predicament. A year had passed since he'd originally discussed the idea with the BBC, but the producer first earmarked for the project had since left for Australia, and they were now reluctant to proceed. 'I thought it was a marvellous idea, and the stories you could get from it were endless, so when asked to produce it, I agreed,' says Graham Scott. A former film editor, Elliot had, aged twenty-three, edited *Brighton Rock* for the Boulting Brothers before joining the BBC as a trainee producer in the early fifties. For a time, Elliot had worked as Graham Scott's assistant in film editing.

By the time they were discussing *Mogul*, Graham Scott had left the Beeb and was working on *The Avengers*, but such was his desire to produce the oil-based show that he quit and re-joined the BBC. 'I had about three months to get *Mogul* on the air, so the schedule was hectic. But we coped and completed thirteen episodes before changing the name to *The Troubleshooters. Mogul* was such a bad title. People confused it with Mobil, the petrol company, and were confused as to what the programme was about – some even thought it was about the Indian occupation by the moguls. For a time, *Delta International* was being considered as an alternative title, which I think was even worse.'

'I had about three months to get *Mogul* on the air, so the schedule was hectic. But we coped and completed thirteen episodes before changing the name to *The Troubleshooters*.'

While working in the petroleum industry, John Elliot had noticed the company employing him held film footage covering every aspect of the profession – ideal material for a drama series about the oil business, he thought. 'We used many of the library shots in the series,' says Graham Scott, who was instrumental in widening the programme's scope to include more internationally influenced storylines, with scripts set in all corners of the world, including Venezuela and Antarctica.

Although slow to excite the viewers, many critics thought it was the best thing since sliced bread, as action regularly switched between high-level decision-making in the boardroom to the grease and guts of the drilling. Incisively written scripts, acted out by a cast boasting names such as Geoffrey Keen, Philip Latham, Ray Barrett, Robert Hardy and Philippa Gail, the show became one of the decade's most popular dramas. 'It was an enjoyable show to work on,' enthuses Graham Scott, who also helped

OPPOSITE: The Cartwright boys on their Ponderosa Ranch in *Bonanza*.

HEADING WEST

Who can forget the rush of westerns that galloped on to our screens with gusto during this period? There was *Outlaws* (1960-2) starring Don Collier as Marshal Will Foreman who, with the aid of his deputies, tried his utmost to rid a district in Oklahoma of its notorious bandits and robbers. Then there was *Cheyenne* and my favourite, *Bonanza*, with the Cartwright boys – well, grown men, actually – who lived on the Ponderosa Ranch, although they were actually from the fifties so strictly speaking don't qualify for inclusion in this book. *The Virginian* does, though. It ran for nine years between 1962 and 1971, first appearing in the UK in 1964. Based on Owen Wister's bestselling novel from 1902 of the same name, it starred James Drury, Doug McClure and Gary Clarke.

launch the Scottish-based series, *This Man Craig*, the first drama series on the newly formed BBC2.

Set north of the border in Strathaird, *This Man Craig* ran for a year between 1966 and 1967, although transmission on the fledgling channel, which experienced limited coverage in its early years, restricted the show's audience figures. The drama was based around physics teacher Ian Craig, whose life in front of the blackboard was portrayed by Glaswegian John Cairney, already a familiar TV face through his appearances on a variety of shows over the previous five years. The fifty-minute stories unfolded in the classrooms and corridors of the town's comprehensive school and, as a one-page brief held in the BBC's archives reveals, the Corporation hoped it would 'reflect a view of Scotland and education in general which will belie the legend of tartan and porridge'.

The first episode was shown on Friday, 7 January 1966 at 8.00 p.m. Throughout the show's lifetime, the production team worked closely with Scottish educational bodies, headmasters and teachers to ensure storylines were as realistic as possible.

Peter Graham Scott recalls the time he headed north to help set up the programme at BBC Scotland: 'Sydney Newman and I were invited to lunch by the Controller of Programmes who wore striped trousers and a morning suit. He said that as it was a special occasion he'd open a bottle. We thought it would be a wonderful bottle of malt whisky and were shocked when he opened a bottle of Bulmer's cider. He asked what we were proposing to do, so I told him we were going to do an hour a week. He replied, "You'll never get an hour a week out of these studios because we've never done an hour of drama." So I said: "Well, they're going to have to." I told him about what we were doing with *Mogul* and asked if he'd seen it. He replied, "I haven't got time to watch programmes." And this was the Controller of Programmes.'

Another drama featuring a Scottish setting was *Dr Finlay's Casebook*, although it was largely shot in a London studio. It was only the filmed inserts from the fictitious Tannochbrae (actually Callander, at the base of Ben Ledi in Perthshire) which actually originated from Scotland.

Its nine-year run began on Thursday, 16 August 1962 and followed the trials and tribulations of a rather green doctor, Alan Finlay, as he took his first tentative steps in general practice, having ditched his ambition of becoming a surgeon.

Dripping in nostalgia, the medical series was set in a rural practice during the 1920s and initially intended to entertain during those cold winter nights with a six-part run, although it was shifted into the summer schedule when a gaping hole was spotted by the Beeb's planning department. The opening episode, 'It's All In The Mind', was applauded by viewers, who enjoyed the period feel and lauded the acting of Bill Simpson as the young Alan Finlay, and Andrew Cruickshank as Dr Cameron.

The series was based on stories by author A. J. Cronin, who'd given up medicine to become a novelist, and reflected a period when doctors were on first-name terms with their patients, still made regular home visits and didn't rely on antibiotics to cure all ills. Considering its longevity, it's hard to believe that the show nearly didn't make it onto our screens. At one point, a three-part drama based on Cronin's own experiences as a doctor was being considered, covering his adventures working in Wales, subsequent exploits as a ship's doctor and the forming of a rural practice in Scotland. The plan, however, was eventually abandoned, the BBC finally deciding that for the show to work, they had to keep faith with Cronin's original characterizations of Doctors Finlay and Cameron, as well as Janet, the housekeeper, all of whom had been clearly detailed in Cronin's autobiography.

Stories from two of Cronin's books, *The Adventures of a Black Bag* and *Further Adventures of a Black Bag*, supplied the storylines for the early episodes and the programme quickly became a ratings winner, collecting several awards, including, in 1965, 'The Best Series of the Year' from the Screenwriters' Guild. The series was also shown abroad in over a dozen countries.

If you liked your dramas hard-hitting and gritty, where the scriptwriters didn't pull their punches, you were probably a *Callan* fan. Here was a guy who led a paradoxical life. On the one hand, he was a British secret service agent-cum-ruthless assassin who'd kill in the line of duty for his employers; on the other, he was a deep-thinking individual constantly wrestling with his conscience and questioning the morality of the tasks he was ordered to carry out. The untitled governmental spy department for which Callan worked was represented by Callan's 'controller' who was known, no matter which of a variety of individuals filled the role, by the sinister codename 'Hunter'.

Viewers were first introduced to the calculating David Callan in an *Armchair Theatre* production, back in February 1967. The character was created by writer James Mitchell and featured in his one-off script, 'A Magnum for Schneider'. Impressing the chiefs at ABC Television, a series was commissioned and shown the same year. Two years later, *Callan* was back on our screens courtesy of Thames Television, the company born in 1968 when ABC and Associated Rediffusion amalgamated after an ITA (Independent Television Authority) reshuffle.

The atmosphere of the seedy underworld in which Callan spent his working life was accentuated by the show's transmission in black and white for the majority of its life.

Callan soon won praise from critics and viewers alike. The show made actor Edward Woodward, who played the agent, a household name, but boasted plenty of other strong characterizations, all adroitly executed by fine actors, including Russell Hunter and Anthony Valentine. Valentine was cast as fellow agent Toby Meres, a role played by Peter Bowles in 'A Magnum for Schneider'. Valentine loved the character:

'He was a character that people absolutely loved because he was a guy who did his own thing and was utterly arbitrary, which viewers liked. He was an incredibly dangerous man: if you stood next to him in a pub and asked an innocent question, he'd either rip your head off or strike up a conversation – you never knew what was going to happen. That's the kind of danger which grips people most of all: the unpredictability. Once a character becomes completely predictable they also become fatally boring.'

The show generated plenty of letters – and not all fan mail. 'There were people who thought it appalling that these people could be working for a government agency – there were people who took it that seriously. Other people thought it was wonderful that a real villain could also be a gentleman who'd attended a public school,' explains Valentine, who believes a number of factors contributed to the show's success. 'There were wonderful performances from Edward Woodward and Russell Hunter, and I think it just gripped people because of its reality. At the same time as being hard and violent, it was also humane because the central character – a brilliantly clever idea – was a man who was doing what he did, not because he wanted to, but because he was forced to, by a government agency.'

A smash hit it certainly was, and the decision to close a series with the possibility that Callan had been killed by Toby Meres provoked an extraordinary response from the public. It was to be the climax of season two, but when the story broke, Thames backed away from their original intention and producer Reginald Collin recorded a new shot of Callan to be tagged onto the broadcast. 'There was this strange graffiti legend that started appearing on walls all over London, which was simply two words: "Callan lives",' recalls Valentine. Valentine will also never forget one particular sequence of location shooting in the Alice Holt Forest, near Guildford, for the episode, 'Heir Apparent', in which Callan and Meres retrieve their new Hunter from behind the Iron Curtain. 'It wasn't funny at the time but in hindsight it had a kind of dark humour to it.' While shepherding a man back into the country, Callan and Meres had to negotiate a minefield. 'We'd been on location for three days in torrential rain, which meant we were up to our knees in mud. Everyone was wet and cold. Because we were supposedly in a minefield, we had to lie down, which made things worse.'

OPPOSITE: Edward Woodward was *Callan*, the assassin with a conscience, while Russell Hunter played his sidekick, Lonely.

SINGING THE PRAISES . . .

What are the special ingredients that when mixed together account for a show's longevity? I guess if we all knew the answer we'd be millionaires by now. Often a programme catering for a particular segment of the overall televisual canvas has a better chance of surviving long-term than a show competing against a dozen others of a similar ilk. *Songs of Praise* is a prime example. It began in 1961 and over four decades later it's still pulling in the punters, providing good value and inspiration for millions. The first instalment was presented from the Tabernacle Baptist Chapel in Cardiff and the show has been travelling the length and breadth of the country ever since. What always brings a smile to my face whenever I tune in is how the churches are always packed with smartly dressed folk in fine voice – I wonder if the congregations are such when normal service resumes? Staying on religious-themed shows, by the end of the decade ITV had launched *Stars on Sunday*. A completely different animal, with an entertainment slant, top names from the world of showbiz would sing hymns as requested by viewers.

In one scene, the enemy, upon spotting the agents, open fire, hitting landmines in the process. 'The special-effects guy, who shall be nameless, had put these electronically-wired charges into the earth, marking them with little red flags which we could see but the camera couldn't. We had to crawl between them, at what was supposed to be a safe distance, while he popped the switch and these things went off and blew a cloud of mud and God knows what into the air – very effective and very dramatic. We had a test run but unfortunately the charges didn't go off. So there we were crawling through this mud literally on our bellies and they didn't go off because they'd been hanging around for three days and were soaked through. Rather than rewiring 500 square yards of English mud, the special-effects man simply put new charges on top of the old ones. Having a cautious nature, I told Ted [Edward Woodward] I was worried about the charges. I thought that not only was the dry charge going to go off but the one underneath would, too. Ted wasn't having this and told the director he wanted to see one exploded. They dragged the special-effects man out, who assured us everything would be all right, but Ted insisted on seeing one go off.'

It's just as well the pair voiced their concerns because both charges detonated and the explosion was so big it fired the charge next to it as well. 'We ended up with a hole you could have lost a mini in – a great chasm opened up. Ted looked at me, before turning to the director and saying: "Right, thank you very much, I'll be in the caravan when you need me."'

One of the nation's best-loved actors, the late John Thaw, will for ever be remembered for playing two of television's greatest coppers: grumpy, beer-loving, Jag-driving Inspector Morse and rough-edged, abrasive Jack Regan in *The Sweeney*. But Thaw's big break on the small screen was in the mid-sixties when, in his twenties, he was cast as Sergeant John Mann in *Redcap*. The show, about the Royal Military Police Special Investigation Branch, ran to twenty-six episodes and was produced by ABC. Mann employed a no-nonsense approach to his investigations, which took him around the world – or that's what the production team would have us believe. The series was actually shot almost entirely in the studio, as Ian Kennedy Martin, who acted as story editor on the series before later creating *The Sweeney*, explains. 'Most of it was made in Studio 2 at Teddington, but occasionally we'd drag the camera some hundred yards into the car park and re-set the studio exterior to represent a street in Limassol or somewhere.'

The idea for *Redcap* arrived in the form of two pages submitted by journalist Jack Bell. The Head of Drama at ABC Television assigned Ian Kennedy Martin and John Bryce to the project. As story editor, Kennedy Martin's brief was to secure the best writers in the country.

'We ended up with a hole you could have lost a mini in – a great chasm opened up.'

Eventually, Charles Wood was commissioned to write two scripts but they were never made, as Kennedy Martin explains: 'The army stepped in. They didn't like the subject matter. One of them was about a bunch of squaddies who fall in love with a tank, and keep polishing it, and when the sergeant rebukes them they use the vehicle to run him over – it was very dark. We thought both scripts were wonderful but our military adviser got a bit nervous and passed them on to someone higher up, who was outraged.'

Kennedy Martin and his colleagues were summoned to a meeting with a general who told them that the army had, for the first time, started advertising on ITV, at great expense. 'He felt that if we intended making thirteen hours of this skulduggery, it would completely cancel out the advertising. We didn't think the scripts would cause any harm but the army didn't agree and we weren't able to use them.'

On the back of securing Charles Wood, even though his scripts were never used, Kennedy Martin was able to attract other good writers, including Michael Ashe and Robert Storey, and once scripts were ready, attention turned to casting. 'John [Thaw] had just come out of drama school and had done a few jobs on telly, but he really was wet behind the ears,' admits Kennedy Martin. 'But on the basis of not a very large part on *The Avengers*, John Bryce [producer], said: "That's our man." I replied: "You're nuts. There are a lot of established actors around here; you're taking a big chance with this guy." Anyhow, John was cast and absolutely wonderful he was, too.'

It was the world of psychiatry that provided the basis for ABC Television's twenty-six-episode show, *The Human Jungle*, which delved into people's problems

BELOW: John Thaw was cast as Sergeant John Mann in *Redcap* despite his lack of TV experience.

UNSEEN FOR TWENTY YEARS

In today's televisual climate, where it seems anything goes as far as content is concerned, it's hard to imagine a programme being banned, but that was the fate of writer and producer Peter Watkins's drama-documentary, *The War Game*. Concerning the country's preparations for and struggles after a nuclear attack, the show was originally due for transmission in 1965. It was halted in its tracks at the last minute, however, by the then Director General, Sir Hugh Greene, who felt the British public would find the images too disturbing. The £70,000 production, containing harrowing images of nuclear war, was eventually given an airing (long after it had been released in cinemas and picked up awards) as part of the BBC's remembrance programme marking the fortieth anniversary of the Hiroshima bomb.

Watkins had first proposed a documentary on the consequences of nuclear warfare, carrying the working title of *After the Bomb*, back in August 1963, but in a memo from Huw Weldon (then Head of Documentary and Music Programmes at the Beeb) to the Director of Television on 31 December 1964, Weldon recalls the time he hired Watkins: 'His [Peter Watkins] over-riding desire was to make an imaginative reconstruction on the subject of the United Kingdom suffering under and reacting to a nuclear attack.' After what Weldon referred to as 'a great deal of anxious thought', he recommended that the documentary went ahead. Weldon had discussed the project with his boss and reached the conclusion that 'so long as there is no security risk and the facts are authentic, the people should be trusted with the truth.' But by 26 November 1965, the BBC had decided not to broadcast the show. A press release stated that the effect of the film had been judged as 'too horrifying for the medium of broadcasting'. Public interest resulted in letters being written to the BBC requesting a transmission, while groups, such as the National Peace Council, asked the Beeb to show the programme to particular organizations, which it later did to invited audiences.

between 1963 and 1965. Playing the lead, Dr Roger Corder, was Prague-born actor Herbert Lom, a veteran of the film industry, although this was his first leading role on the small screen. So realistic was his portrayal that many viewers, believing he was a real-life psychiatrist, wrote to him asking for help in sorting out their own problems.

Lom relished his role as a doctor of the mind: 'I was interested in psychiatry – I think all actors are. I knew that psychiatrists weren't particularly popular among the population because many people didn't understand what psychiatry was all about. So I hoped the series would help people realize that psychiatrists are nice doctors simply trying to help.'

As was the norm in series of that period, all the doctor's cases were solved – such was the unquestionable brilliance of this man! Lom, however, would rather have seen his character fail occasionally, thereby enhancing the show's realism.

'Some very good colleagues became my patients,' he remembers. 'I remember Dr Corder saw one patient, a young woman, who had a compulsion to take off her clothes in public places because of her illness. The woman in question was played by Joan Collins. Other very good actors played the patient of the week. The only criticism I had was I cured them all in an hour, so to speak. I begged with the producers to let me have one or two where I failed, because that would have been more realistic, but they wouldn't agree. All my patients had to be cured – that's television, I guess.'

The series was made at Pinewood, which meant a trek for actors living in the capital. Rather than spend three hours each day travelling to and from work, Lom decided to kip at the studios. 'It was very tiring because they scheduled me in such a way that I was needed every day of the week. Although I had a driver, I decided not to drive home in the evening, preferring to sleep in the studio instead. I had a bed put in my dressing room and spent the night there. An actor's life!'

Lom was disappointed the series didn't make it in the States. 'The people who tried selling the programme to America were lovely but didn't have the right contacts. We could only sell it as a summer replacement, so in the end it ran on some television stations but only as a substitute when the main programmes were having a break.'

Meanwhile, from Yorkshire Television in 1968, *Gazette*'s dozen episodes concerning the owner of a local paper, James Hadleigh, led to over fifty episodes of a spin-off, *Hadleigh*, which outshone its predecessor when it ran from 1969 until 1976. A campaigner on behalf of the underdog, the urbane squire of Melford Park was played by Gerald Harper, who'd recently been seen as Adam Adamant.

Harper wasn't upset when *Adam Adamant Lives!* came to an end because he felt that staying with the character too long would lead to him becoming typecast. And whereas that show hadn't lived up to expectations, *Hadleigh* was the antithesis of the BBC's adventure series. 'It was unbelievably successful. One year, I was even voted more popular than Tom Jones!' Harper says with a smile.

He remembers receiving the call offering him the part in *Gazette*. 'They said: "It's not a huge part because it's all about the local newspaper and you're the owner who lives in a house up the hill. You just come in every now and again and have a row with the editor. But it means you'll have to go to Yorkshire." I'd worked so hard on *Adam Adamant Lives!*, the idea of not having a big part appealed to me hugely.

'So we did a series of *Gazette*. At the end, the producer told me they'd decided to throw away the *Gazette* angle and continue just with my character. I said: "Oh, dear." So there I was on every page of the script again, which meant having to learn seventy pages every fortnight. But at least *Hadleigh* was taken seriously and made well. They got the best directors, hired good writers and produced it well.'

ABOVE: Playing a psychiatrist, Herbert Lom had to deal with Joan Collins's compulsion to strip off in *The Human Jungle*.

Now here's a question for you. Which Francis Durbridge-created sleuth from the 1930s became the BBC's most expensive crime series when it transferred from radio to television in 1969? The answer is *Paul Temple*, which saw Francis Matthews playing the amateur detective, and Ros Drinkwater as his wife. Running to fifty-two episodes during its two-year life, the show's total budget was an astonishing £630,000 – a paltry sum by today's standards, perhaps, but a huge figure back in the sixties.

Parkin's Patch, meanwhile, didn't cost anywhere near the kind of money the Beeb splashed out. Yorkshire Television's series from 1969 concerning the day-to-day incidents in the life of country bobby PC Moss Parkin was a gentle study of policing in a rural patch in Yorkshire. The

'It was very tiring because they scheduled me in such a way that I was needed every day of the week. Although I had a driver, I decided not to drive home in the evening, preferring to sleep in the studio instead.'

173

star of the show was actor John Flanagan, who nowadays earns his living as a scriptwriter on shows such as *Heartbeat*. When he jumped into his panda car in 1969 for the first of the half-hour episodes, he was fresh out of drama school and very green. 'I left drama school in 1968 and worked at the Bristol Old Vic for six months. I'd done a couple of small roles on television, but *Parkin's Patch* was my first series,' says Flanagan, who was twenty-two at the time. Although only six instalments were originally planned, the programme extended to twenty-six, but Flanagan believes poor scheduling eventually led to it being dropped. 'In those days on the network, the stations weren't always in sync. There was a fractured showing of the series and I think it had an effect on the overall viewing figures. It's much easier for all concerned if a programme has a regular slot.'

Parkin's Patch helped put Flanagan's name on the acting map, but straight after the show he returned to the theatre 'to learn the craft of acting properly'. He says: 'I enjoyed the six months of television but it wasn't entirely all I wanted to do. Granada Television ran a theatre company, which is unheard of these days, so I joined them after playing PC Parkin.'

But Flanagan will never forget the first day of shooting on the Yorkshire moors because it coincided with the start of the grouse-shooting season. 'Unfortunately this had been overlooked. We went up to this wonderful moorland location to do the exteriors – you couldn't get a more peaceful location – and the sound guy, smiling away, said: "No problems for me today: it's not on the flight path and there are no cars around." We started shooting but every now and again had to stop because these guys were banging away with their guns all day long. It was intermittent and you never knew when it was going to happen. By the end of the day, the sound guy was pulling his hair out.'

On reflection, John Flanagan believes the job arrived too soon in his career. 'If I'd had another year or two before it happened, I'd probably have appreciated it better and been in a better position to make more of it. I was still learning what television was about but had the responsibility of leading the series while at the same time having no idea what I was doing – it was a brave piece of casting. When it ended I was relieved that the strain of carrying it, which got to me a bit, was over.

'I then decided to return to the theatre and learn how to do the job properly. I always felt that the series had the potential to run a little while but clearly something of that nature wouldn't have the legs of other series, simply because you were going to run out of credible stories.'

A slightly different approach to the traditional 'cops and robbers' story was provided by London Weekend Television's *The Gold Robbers*. A multi-million-pound bullion snatch and the efforts of Detective Chief

CALLING ALL SPORTS FANS

The BBC's *Grandstand* has become a veteran in the world of sports coverage. While some titles have failed to last the distance, the Beeb's flagship sporting show is the marathon runner of the genre. Its stamina and freshness have seen it become the world's longest-running live sports programme, but as it leapt from its starting blocks in 1958, it's not strictly for inclusion in this book. It largely had a clear field until ITV dished up their own live sports show in the shape of *World of Sport*. Of course, Richard 'Dickie' Davies (below) became the face of *World of Sport* but in the beginning it was Eamonn *'This Is Your Life'* Andrews who sat in the presenter's chair, ably assisted by a host of experts. These included Freddie Trueman and Jimmy Hill providing views on the latest cricket and football stories while John Rickman gave his tips on the day's racing, and journalists Peter Lorenzo and Ian Wooldridge were always around with their forthright opinions. Arguably the working man's sports show, it didn't just focus on football and horse racing but also wrestling, darts and a host of other sports.

Football addicts, meanwhile, couldn't wait for Saturday nights and *Match of the Day*. It launched in 1964 on the newborn BBC2, but by the time the World Cup in 1966 got underway, the programme had switched to BBC1. It began life when the BBC's Bryan Cowgill arranged with the Football League for a forty-five-minute recording of one of the afternoon's matches to be screened. Kenneth Wolstenholme and Wally Barnes were in charge of the microphone for the commentaries in the early days, and although it has evolved over the decades, it's yet another shining example of the Beeb striking gold.

Superintendent Cradock, played by Peter Vaughan, to find those responsible was the premise for thirteen episodes in 1969. Writer John Whitney recalls being asked to come up with the idea. 'The programme controller rang me one weekend and asked if I wanted £5,000. I told him I was always happy to oblige. He wanted an idea by Monday which was to do with crime and would last thirteen episodes. He wanted me to start working on it and so I did, and he ended up buying the idea, which followed the story of each character who'd taken part in the major gold robbery, and what became of them.'

John Whitney was a busy man during the sixties – and still is. In 1963, he was employed as script editor, together with his writing partner, Geoffrey Bellman, on ATV's *The Plane Makers*, which revolved around the aviation industry and the factory floor of the fictitious aircraft manufacturers Scott Furlong. Screened between 1963 and 1965, this popular drama was commissioned by the station's chief, Lew Grade, who originally wanted a series about the manufacture of telephones! When telephones weren't deemed sexy enough, attention switched to the aviation business and *The Plane Makers* was born. Head of the fictional company was the merciless John Wilder, expertly played by Patrick Wymark, who went on to greater things when, after two years, the company collapsed and he joined the board of a merchant bank in the offshoot series, *The Power Game*. The new show became even more popular than its predecessor, following the exploits of Wilder, who ultimately became a member of the Foreign Office. Riding high in the ratings, the programme came to an abrupt end when its leading man, Patrick Wymark, died of a heart attack while in Australia.

Returning to the world of aviation in 1962, the then London Airport (now better known as London Heathrow Airport) was regarded as being at the crossroads of international air travel. The airport was also the supposed headquarters of a fictitious organization called the International Air Security Board, the codename for which was the title of the series – *Zero One*. The series began in September with Nigel Patrick cast in the lead role as Zero One's chief investigator, Alan Garnett. While most of the location work was shot at London Airport, interior scenes were completed at the MGM Studios at Borehamwood, Hertfordshire, which housed a complete airliner's flight-deck for filming purposes, courtesy of eight airlines and four aircraft manufacturers who kindly supplied parts for the set's construction. The series was an idea developed by Donald Fish, an airline security expert and former police officer, based on a book he had written, *Airline Detective*. Over a period of three years up to 1965, thirty-nine episodes were made by the BBC, the first series benefiting from the appearance of stars such as Cecil Parker and Margaret Rutherford, who might otherwise have been unavailable but for an Equity dispute that prevented members of the actors' union from working for independent television early in 1962.

One quirky crime drama to emerge from the anthology series *Detective*, which in 1964 (and again four years later) set out to showcase some of the best crime stories around, was *Cluff*. The BBC commissioned a series of six stories about the north country detective and within four weeks of the transmission of the first show in April 1964 the audience

BELOW: Leslie Sands was pampered when he played a rich industrialist in Granada's 1969 drama *Two Feet off the Ground*, a feeling he never enjoyed in *Cluff*.

had risen from 7 million to 12 million. A further thirteen episodes were swiftly commissioned for transmission from May the following year. Set in the Yorkshire Dales, the series had Leslie Sands, already a familiar face on television thanks to his role as Superintendent Miller in *Z Cars*, playing Detective Sergeant Caleb Cluff, whose constant companion was Clive, his faithful dog.

Another sleuth with a four-legged friend was Detective Inspector Steve Bollinger, played by Louis Hayward in ABC's 1961 production, *The Pursuers*. Bollinger's dog, Ivan, helped him to tackle crime on the grimy streets of London. Thirty-nine episodes were produced before Bollinger and Ivan, suffering from dwindling ratings, were pensioned off.

While Bollinger was interested in crime in the capital, Danny Scipio – played by Italian actor Stelio Candelli – embarked on a worldwide crusade against the Mafia in *Vendetta*. Danny was the sole applicant when a Rome-based commission advertised for someone to head its mission to fight the Mafia, an appointment he accepted partly as a response to seeing his parents murdered when he was a child of ten. His adventures saw him jetting off to all parts of the world, heightening the show's chances of exposure abroad in the process.

Created by Tudor Gates and Brian Degas, *Vendetta* sprang from a meeting between Degas and the BBC's Head of Drama during which they discussed ideas for a new series. When Degas informed his writing partner, Tudor Gates, that a show about the Mafia had been suggested, Gates recalls: 'I couldn't see how we could make a series about the Mafia work. Then Brian came up with a newspaper cutting about someone who'd been appointed in Sicily as a kind of anti-Mafia commissioner; I suddenly said, "That's it, let's write a story about the man who fights the Mafia." And that was the birth of Danny Scipio.'

Gates was instrumental in casting the lead role. 'We went out to Italy – where we'd been writing films – and found Stelio Candelli. We interviewed a number of actors but once many of them knew it was about the Mafia, they said: "No, thank you" and dropped out. It was extraordinary.'

American crime drama was as big in the sixties as it is today and one of the most popular imports was *A Man Called Ironside*, about a wheelchair-bound detective played by Raymond Burr. Burr had become a household name and had made a fortune playing lawyer Perry Mason before portraying the crippled Robert Ironside, whose paralysis was the result of a would-be assassin's bullet in the spine. Ironside did not, however, let his disability prevent him from trying to clean up the streets of San Francisco, persuading the police department to let him work as a special consultant to the force. The series, titled simply *Ironside* in the States, was a hit across the pond and, in

> 'Let's write a story about the man who fights the Mafia. And that was the birth of Danny Scipio.'

A BREAKTHROUGH IN SCIENCE

For the scientifically minded, *Tomorrow's World* hit all the right notes when it launched in 1965. Fronted, initially, by Raymond Baxter (left), it was billed as the 'TV magazine which reports on what's new today for those interested in tomorrow'. And its first instalment didn't waste time on piddling little ideas, exploring instead one of the most exciting recent discoveries – the laser. Baxter reported on its use in eye surgery, and viewers were allowed to look over the surgeon's shoulder during two operations at Moorfields Eye Hospital. The *Radio Times* was in serious mode when it previewed the opening slice of the series, stating: 'These programmes will be concerned with the uses of scientific research, as well as its excitement; and with the social patterns of industrial change as well as its techniques. They are programmes about the future – your future!'

turn, entertained British viewers, too, when it received its first airing. So realistic was Burr in the role that viewers wrote to the American studios passing on their wishes to Burr for a speedy recovery, not realizing the wheelchair was simply a prop.

Other imports from the States included NBC's 1961 series, *87th Precinct*, which was inspired by the work of American author, Ed McBain, and utilized Manhattan as the backdrop for the hard-hitting detective series, while New York was chosen for *The Defenders*, an outstanding example of American drama at its best. The father-and-son law firm, Preston and Preston, took on plenty of tough and topical, socially relevant cases during the four years it was broadcast. With incisive writing, sharp direction and adroit acting from E. G. Marshall as Lawrence Preston and Robert Reed as his son, Kenneth, the show quickly established itself in the television schedules and attracted a host of well-known guest stars, including Robert Redford, Gene Hackman and Dustin Hoffman. The programme's creator, Reginald Rose, said at the time: 'Our stories deal more with human emotions than they do with technical points of the law. Each one is built from a character with a real-life problem, not from a fancy and intricate

GOING *NATIONWIDE*

If you liked keeping abreast of events happening around the UK, *Nationwide* was the programme for you. Beginning in 1969, the popular current affairs programme claimed the early evening slot on BBC1 formerly held by the *Tonight* show. Pushing the then primitive broadcasting technology to its limits with numerous live links to the various regions, the programme covered every type of story imaginable, including that of the famous skateboarding duck. *Nationwide* ran until the early eighties, regularly attracting audiences above 10 million, and among its many presenters were Frank Bough, Sue Lawley, Sue Cook, Hugh Scully, John Stapleton and Valerie Singleton.

Michael Barratt (below), the show's original host, describes how *Nationwide* came to be: 'Paul Fox, who was then controller of BBC1, had a problem because he couldn't retain an audience after six in the evening. He tried all kinds of things, like quiz shows, but audience figures always fell away. So he turned to a genius by the name of Derrick Amoore to sort the matter out. What Derrick quickly realized was that they were getting a big enough audience so long as the opt-out regional programmes were on air. He realized there was a strong regional loyalty so puzzled over how to capitalize on this and came up with *Nationwide*, which would embrace all the loyalties of regional audiences and build on that. The programme was plugged in to eleven different regional programmes.

'The kind of stories we covered also reflected regional thinking. Every morning we had a meeting and talked to news editors in the regions. They'd give us their leading stories and every now and again we'd say: "Hey, that's a good story for a wider audience." We'd move from a story like the skateboarding duck straight to a live interview with the Prime Minister and have a serious discussion. We could move seamlessly from light frothy stuff to serious stories – and we covered all the major stories of the day.

'From the beginning [9 September 1969] it was very chaotic, and was transmitted three evenings a week. We were pushing the boundaries of technology, and the idea of having all these studios live on air was a major exercise, although we did get a lot of egg on our faces. We'd, say, head off to Edinburgh for a contribution and find we had a lot of wavy lines and a voice. We came very close in the first couple of months to being taken off air because we were almost a laughing stock with the things that went wrong, but that was purely because no one had tried the format before – the programme was very brave. It eventually became, in my view, the most professionally adept programme in terms of its production values that I've ever worked on.'

While the live links provided peculiar technical problems all of their own, the odd hiccup in the studio was not unknown, either, as Barratt recalls:

'I worked on the programme for eight years but in programme number two [Wednesday, 10 September 1969] I was introducing an item, which was on film, but a breakdown meant we couldn't show it – there was just a blank screen. In those days, we had a telephone on the desk, which rang, so I picked it up and a voice said: "We've lost the film." They then put the phone down. I had an agonizing few minutes to fill. Later on, that wouldn't have been a problem because I could have selected some viewers' letters and read them out, but we didn't have any because it was only day two. The only thing on my desk, which was out of view, was a clock, so I finished up by saying: "Now, a lot of you have called asking what I've got on my desk." And I proceeded to tell the viewers, even though, of course, no one had actually called.'

Nationwide came to an end in the early eighties, by which time the BBC clearly felt that the show had run its course, although it had changed hugely in character by then, as Barratt explains: 'I left in 1977 and there was a view later on that it should be made more serious. I felt that it lost its way.'

plot in which the characters are almost incidental.' The winner of numerous Emmys in the States, the series wasn't afraid to confront thorny issues in its storylines, a forceful approach that occasionally saw the programme court controversy, but which was one of its strengths.

How many fans of *Columbo* remember that Peter Falk's first major TV role was in 1966, three years before donning the grubby raincoat and puffing on all those cigars? In *The Trials of O'Brien*, Falk played a lawyer who wasn't one of the legal profession's high flyers and was beset with

BELOW: Prior to starring in *Columbo*, Peter Falk played a troubled lawyer in *The Trials of O'Brien*.

problems both professional and personal. And do you remember *The Nurses*, which followed the dedicated staff of the fictitious New York hospital, the Alden General, or *Ripcord,* about commercial parachuting, with Ted McKeever (played by Larry Pennell) and Jim Buckley (Ken Curtis) tackling seemingly impossible missions by venturing where no man, or machine, was able to reach?

Historical drama had never been portrayed in quite the same way before *The Borderers*, reportedly the first action-adventure series made in colour. The closest homegrown television came to producing a western, *The Borderers* transported viewers back to the sixteenth century. Peter Graham Scott produced the show, which was set on the frontiers of England and Scotland when, as the programme's promotional booklet stated, the region was 'rife with violence, cattle-rustling and feud'. The booklet boasted that a team of experts worked on historical research, while the cast included such reliable talents as Michael Gambon and Joe Brady.

Derek Ware was the stunt expert employed on the series. 'It was an intriguing idea, with a large budget by BBC standards. It was well cast, too, but I think the production staff had no idea of the difficulties involved when filming with horses, particularly highland ponies; they're ideal for traversing the rugged terrain dividing Scotland and England, but their natural gait is a dog trot rather than the canter or gallop that gives the western its "oomph"!

'Moreover, any actor anxious to secure a role in a production that requires good riding ability may tend to be economical with the truth as to his or her actual proficiency. The result is much precious time is wasted when, in front of a camera, on the back of the most unpredictable animal in the world, they simply fall off or keep being carried away in a direction other than the one the director is expecting them to take. Although I had a stunt team of six to perform the risky work or act as riding doubles, no contingency had been made for duplicate costumes, footwear or headgear. Thus, when a stuntman had to substitute for an actor the pair had to share the same set of clothes.'

Drama was undoubtedly one of the most prolific genres in television during the decade, with a myriad series coming off the production line. The surfeit of productions, which came in all guises, meant plenty of work for the industry's thespians. Actor George Layton, who later found fame in the small-screen version of *Doctor in the House*, was out of work

> '...much precious time is wasted when, in front of a camera, on the back of the most unpredictable animal in the world, they simply fall off or keep being carried away in a direction other than the one the director is expecting them to take.'

AROUND THE WORLD 1969

The decade finished on a high note – very high, in fact – when the first man set foot on the moon. Neil Armstrong clambered down from *Apollo 11*, tested the lunar landscape and uttered those immortal words: 'One small step for man, one giant leap for mankind.' America had finally overtaken the Soviet Union in space. Colour TV was rolled out across the entire ITV network (although some had dipped their toe in the water the previous year) in November, with the make-up artists warning readers of *TV Times* magazine of some of the things they might expect to spot, courtesy of colour transmissions. Their warnings included: 'Nicotine-stained fingers really stand out', 'bags under eyes are more prominent' and 'wigs are easy to spot'.

when offered the role of Eustace Madden, a beatnik, in *Swizzlewick*. Following the capricious dealings of a local council in a fictitious Midlands town, the twice-weekly BBC serial ran for thirteen episodes in 1964. 'The guy who was going to play the character suddenly got a duodenal ulcer and was rushed off to hospital so couldn't do the part,' says Layton. 'This girl who was in it – I can't remember her name – was also represented by my agent and said it would be ideal for me. My agent arranged an interview and I whizzed up to Birmingham, where the series was being made, and ended up appearing in it for six months. It was a terrific idea, way ahead of its time. It was written in restoration style and took a satirical view on local government. But then Mary Whitehouse came on the scene and, being election year, it couldn't be as satirical and it dissipated. It must have been heartbreaking for David Turner, the scriptwriter, because it was a great idea, a real knock at local government.'

Save for a host of dramatic characterizations earlier in his career in British movies from the fifties and sixties, the name Sid James is synonymous with comedy – *Hancock's Half Hour* and *Bless This House* being two shows for which he is fondly remembered. James was, perhaps, a less obvious choice for the lead role of cabbie Sid Stone in *Taxi!* because, although there were strands of comedy running through the storylines, it was regarded by many as drama. But Ted Willis, editor and writer of five of the thirteen scripts, conducted research for the series by spending weeks with London cabbies, telling a journalist on the *Radio Times*: 'The character Sid plays is a bit of an adventurer, always getting involved in other people's problems. This is essentially a drama series although there is a good deal of natural comedy arising from the situations.'

Other titles that might get the old memory cells working are the period drama, *The Forsyte Saga*, which was transmitted over six months in 1967 and boasted a cast of, among others, Kenneth More, Nyree Dawn Porter and Susan Hampshire. This glittering saga from John Galsworthy had viewers glued to their seats for the entirety of its twenty-one hours of screening. BBC2's *The Revenue Men* featured the exploits of investigators from Customs and Excise during its twenty-five episodes (1967-8), while one of the decade's more unusual thrillers was Granada's four-part *The Corridor People*, which presented the madcap schemes of Syrie Van Epp, played by Elizabeth Shepherd, and security agents Phil Scrotty and Kronk (Gary Cockrell and John Sharp). The world of forensic science was behind the success of *The Expert*, four series being made between 1968 and 1976. In the Warwickshire-based series, Marius Goring played Dr John Hardy who led a busy life employing his skilled techniques to solve crimes committed in the nearby industrial cities of the Midlands.

OPPOSITE: Two of the regular Pan's People *Top of the Pops* dancers are painted gold before filming a routine.

WELCOME TO *TOP OF THE POPS*!

A television transmission from a converted church in Manchester on New Year's Day, 1964, marked the beginning of a television institution. Forty-two years later, it's still entertaining millions with its look at what's hot on the music scene. The first edition was presented by Jimmy Saville and set in motion by The Rolling Stones' rendition of their number-thirteen hit, 'I Wanna Be Your Man'. For a show intending to run for just seven weeks, it hasn't done badly, has it? Back in the sixties it was a fraught, albeit exciting show to work on. In order to plan for the live broadcast on Wednesday evening, the producer predicted what he thought the charts, which weren't published until Tuesday afternoon, would be. With the use of his crystal ball, he'd provisionally book artists, only for final alterations to be made at the eleventh hour.

WE'RE ALL GOING ON A SUMMER HOLIDAY

Tour operators were a firmly established feature of high streets all over the UK by the sixties and, although the destinations offered as package holidays were still fairly restricted, the jet age had brought affordable air travel within the grasp of the average holidaymaker. The vagaries of the British climate and the uninviting prospect of eating soggy chips in the rain at Margate, or at any other British seaside resort, also combined to drive people abroad. People were flocking to the passport offices and packing their sun cream, sunglasses and swimming costumes for their well-earned annual break. Keen to exploit this cultural shift, the BBC launched *Holiday 69*, a show which, although it has changed cosmetically over the decades, is still running today, affording viewers the same basic structure.

Back in 1969, it was the smiling face of Cliff Michelmore (right), later to be replaced by Frank Bough, who showed us, warts and all, some of the packages available to the new breed of traveller. Providing such practical advice as how to book a holiday or how to decipher the minefield of travel brochure price lists, the programme capitalized on the changing attitude towards venturing abroad for one's vacation. For the first time, here was a show which guided the nervous viewers, taking them by the hand to show them what was available: a practical look at holidaying at home as well as abroad. Yet it wasn't the first travel show. There had been others on radio, and travel-based shows on the box, too.

The inimitable Alan Whicker, who didn't seem to suffer the usual creased-holiday-clothes look the rest of us endured, began his global travels in 1959, while the holiday escapades of the Dimbleby family – broadcaster Richard, his wife, Dilys, and their two sons, David and Jonathan – were enormously popular. Dimbleby's series of five adventures from the late fifties, *Passport*, followed the family's jaunts to various European destinations. Leading the pack, Richard issued everyone with chores, addressing his wife in one episode with: "Now darling, you're the expert on all forms of shopping, so will you go and find out what the prices are, and we'll meet later, OK?" David and Jonathan weren't simply speechless bystanders either and were actively involved, whether they wanted to be or not.

A sequel, *No Passport*, followed in 1960, but nine years later the arrival of *Holiday 69* introduced a new-style magazine format. Cliff Michelmore believes the programme arrived on the scene at just the right moment. 'There had been holiday programmes on the radio – I'd even worked on some, but with *Holiday 69* we happened to hit when the tour market was opening out.' Michelmore admits he didn't intend staying with the programme long. 'I said to Tom Savage [the producer], when he asked me to do it, that I'd do it for a year or so. I ended up staying seventeen years. I wasn't that keen on being away. I had two young children – m son was twelve, my daughter ten – so I didn't want to be travelling the world, although that's what happened. I also had a lot of work in other spheres, so didn't need to be away.'

While chatting with his mate Robin Day at the Garrick Club in London, Michelmore discovered that, apparently, he hadn't been first choice. 'It had just been announced in the papers that I was going to be presenting the series, and Robin nudged me and said: "Do you know, Tom Savage asked me to do that." I asked why he hadn't accepted and he replied: "I had too many other things on, like you have – I'm surprised you're doing it." I told him I was only going to do it for a year or so, to help get it going.'

There were thirteen instalments in the first season, with Tom Savage clearly indicating his intentions for the series. In a memo, dated 5 September 1968, to Aubrey Singer, then Head of Features Group, he explained: 'I do feel that my job is to interest and encourage the audience to be more aware of the basic facts of all types of holidays, and to perhaps be a little more adventurous, whether it be aqualung diving under Swanage pier or just lying in the sun in Torremolinos rather than Bournemouth at, as often as not, the same price!' It's amazing what was classed as 'adventurous' in those days.

Instrumental in the launch and life of the show was John Carter, then travel editor of *The Times* and secretary of the Guild of Travel Writers, who had badgered the BBC for years to launch a travel show. Then, Gordon Watkins, with whom Carter had already conversed, phoned and said he'd reconsidered Carter's idea and would put him in touch with producer Tom Savage, who'd been left with a hole in his television schedules after a programme idea had collapsed. Over lunch they discussed Carter's plans for a programme which was, effectively, an extension of the travel pages from the newspapers. Between them they devised a format but, as Carter explains, there was a major hurdle which had to be overcome if the show was to succeed. 'It would only work if we could mention brand names and prices. It was no good showing people a weekend break in France and then come back to the studio for Cliff to say: "You can get information about that from your travel agent."' This was the big stumbling block but eventually a decision was made at governor level which gave the go-head. For the Beeb to be seen promoting commercial products smacked of

advertising, and that hadn't happened on the BBC before. A pilot programme was shown to a sample audience in BBC's Broadcasting House to gauge reaction. 'People thought it was interesting but they were very worried that the BBC was going commercial with advertising – they were anxious that we should be editorially independent,' explains Carter.

In the early days of the programme, pre-autocue, Carter remembers using a 'primitive system' called Portaprompt. He recalls: 'The guy who did it had a typewriter which typed huge characters on big rolls of paper, which were positioned on a sort of music stand; Cliff would look at the camera but his script was just slightly left of the lens, which someone would be winding up gradually. On occasions the stand would slowly start to collapse.'

Not everyone was enamoured of the programme. While viewers and many critics liked the series, the travel industry wasn't so chuffed. 'The travel trade hated it because where necessary we criticized products. No one approached me personally because I was involved in the programme, but they spoke to travel writers on other newspapers and magazines saying things like: "If this sort of thing goes on, we're going to have to reconsider our position regarding advertising in your publication." So there was a certain amount of pressure from other parts of the media to get us to tone it down a bit because we were rocking the boat, but we didn't.' Eventually the doubters realized that if they could get their product on screen, even if the team was slightly critical, it could still generate good business.'

The programme catered for those inquisitive Brits who were interested in experiencing, perhaps for the first time, holidays abroad. 'Suddenly people were going to Spain and coming back saying: "Not only did the two weeks, including the flight out and back, cost less than the two weeks we spent last year at Blackpool, but the sun was guaranteed, we had a lovely balcony in our room overlooking the sea and we had our own bathroom!"' says Carter. 'I spoke to plenty of tour operators at the time and they'd tell me that people would arrive at a hotel, pick up their bags, get their room key and then stand around looking confused because they'd never been in a lift and didn't know how to work it. It sounds crazy now, but that's the way people were.'

Holidaying abroad was certainly a big adventure.

ACKNOWLEDGEMENTS

I'd like to thank the people who helped during the research and writing of this book, especially those who gave up time to be interviewed or to consign their memories of this bygone era to paper or email, including Harold Snoad, David Croft, Jimmy Perry, Norman Hudis, Sir Roger Moore, Anna Home, Joan Hickson, Alison Prince, David Ellison, John Ryan, Priscilla Ryan, Isabel Ryan, Daphne Robertson, Keith Chatfield, John Bennett, Ian Kennedy Martin, Troy Kennedy Martin, John Whitney, Barrie Heads, Cliff Michelmore, John Carter, Brian Clemens, Honor Blackman, Leonard White, Pat Keysell, Wilf Lunn, Bob Holness, Hazel Adair, Ivor Jay, Peter Ling, Brian Cant, Anne Aston, Oliver Postgate, Peter Firmin, Richard Thorp, Gordon Murray, Anthony Valentine, Verity Lambert, Roberta Leigh, Richard Bradford, Michael Sharland, Irene Shubik, Sandra Payne, Cyril Frankel, Kenneth Cope, Kenneth Kendall, Louis Marks, Peter Halliday, Michael Hayes, John Flanagan, Michael Barrett, Gerry Anderson, Valerie Leon, David Bernstein, Peter Graham Scott, Geoffrey Keen, Michael Bond, Carole Hersee, Jane Rossington, Tony Adams, Lynette McMorrough, Angus Lennie, Tudor Gates, Peter Purves and, once again, Derek Ware.

I'd also like to thank Jaz Wiseman and Andrew Pixley for casting their eyes over some of the chapters to ensure the material is as accurate as possible. People who helped in other ways include Al Samujh, Sue Jay, Gareth Owen, James Codd at the BBC Written Archives, Hilary Johnson, my agent Jeffrey Simmons, and Lindsay Davies, Judith Palmer and Rod Green at Michael O'Mara.

BIBLIOGRAPHY

The following publications, websites and internal BBC correspondence have proved useful sources of information.

BOOKS:
Bentley, Chris, *The Complete Gerry Anderson*
  (Reynolds and Hearn, Richmond, ISBN: 1903111412)
Croft, David, *You Have Been Watching . . .*
  (BBC, London, ISBN: 0563487399)
Fulton, Roger, *The Encyclopedia of Science Fiction*
  (Boxtree, London, ISBN: 1852832770)
Haining, Peter, *On Call With Doctor Finlay*
  (Boxtree, London, ISBN: 1852834714)
Lewisohn, Mark, Radio Times *Guide to TV Comedy*
  (BBC, London, ISBN: 0563369779)
Little, Daran, *The Coronation Street Story*
  (Boxtree, London, ISBN: 1852834641)
Simper, Paul, *The Saint*
  (Chameleon, London, ISBN: 0233991026)
Vahimagi, Tise, *British Television*
  (Oxford University Press, Oxford, ISBN: 0198183364)
Webber, Richard, *Whatever Happened To The Likely Lads?*
(Orion, London, ISBN: 0752818155)
Webber, Richard, *A Celebration of* The Good Life
  (Orion, London, ISBN: 0752818309)
Webber, Richard, *Dad's Army – A Celebration*
  (Virgin, London, ISBN: 0753503077)

WEBSITES:
www.itc-classics.com
www.imdb.com
www.sixtiescity.com
www.nostalgiacentral.com
www.televisionheaven.co.uk
www.toonhound.com
www.bbc.co.uk
www.homepages.tesco.net/~space.patrol
www.theavengers.tv/forever

BBC WRITTEN ARCHIVE SOURCES:
Various policy and production files at BBC Written Archives at Caversham, Berkshire, were accessed during the research period. Material and quotes were used from files in sections T16 (Television Policy), T12 (Television Light Entertainment), T5 (Television Drama), T14 (Television Outside Broadcasts) and volumes of the *Radio Times*.

INDEX

*(page numbers in italic type
refer to pictures)*